MOTHER, BROTHER, LOVER

# Mother, Brother, Lover
*Selected Lyrics*

JARVIS COCKER

*faber and faber*

First published in 2011
by Faber and Faber Ltd
Bloomsbury House
74–77 Great Russell Street
London WC1B 3DA

Typeset by Ian Bahrami
Printed in England by TJ International Ltd, Padstow, Cornwall

A CIP record for this book
is available from the British Library

ISBN 978–0–571–28190–9 (cased edition)

ISBN 978–0–571–28201–2 (limited edition)

10 9 8 7 6 5 4 3 2 1

*To K. S. – for allowing it to happen*
  *and*
*S. C. R. – for getting the ball rolling in the first place*

# Contents

# Introduction

I never intended to be a lyricist. I had wanted to be a pop star from about the age of eight (that's probably when I first saw the Beatles' film *Help!*) but, when I finally managed to cajole three school friends into being in a group with me back in 1978, we were too inept to play other people's songs and so had to write our own material. Because it was my group and I was the singer, I ended up having to write the words. So I found myself in the position that a lot of songwriters start off in: you don't particularly want to do the job but because a song isn't really a song until it's got some lyrics, it's down to you to write them. And this kind of 'Aw, Mum, do I really have to do my homework?' attitude stays with you throughout the years. If you ever have the misfortune to be in a recording studio where work has ground to a halt, it won't be because the drummer has 'drummer's block' or the guitarist has 'guitarist's block', only writers get 'blocked'. Many of the lyrics in this book were hastily written the night before a recording session because I'd been putting off writing them until the very last minute. It's strange that the most intelligible part of a song – the words, those things that people use to communicate with each other all the time – should be seen as the most boring and chore-like aspect of the songwriting process by musicians themselves. And I think that's down to a very simple fact: the words to a song are not that important. Not *that* important but you've got to have them anyway – they're a contractual obligation, a necessary evil, an afterthought.

Take an undisputed rock classic like 'Louie, Louie' by the Kingsmen. The lyrics to that song are so indecipherable that they actually prompted an FBI investigation into their allegedly obscene content back in the early 1960s. (It seems that people could hear such immortal lines as 'I felt my boner in her hair'.) After a thirty-one-month-long investigation, the FBI concluded that they were 'unable to interpret any of the wording in the record'. In other words – you can't tell a word of what the singer is singing and *it doesn't matter*.

But once you've realised that the words are not so important then the real fun of lyric-writing can begin. If nobody's listening you can say whatever you want. My first attempts roughly coincided with my first romantic dealings with the opposite sex. I was struck by the massive discrepancy between the way relationships were depicted in the songs I'd heard on the radio and the way I was experiencing them in real life (could have been my technique, I suppose.) So I decided to try and redress the balance, to put in all the awkward bits and the fumblings. Maybe lyrics weren't that important to a song's success but I realised that they *were* important to me. I was always looking for something in them that generally wasn't there. I had loved pop music from an early age and now I wanted it to go through puberty with me – so I ended up documenting my puberty through pop music itself. This became the blueprint for the way I worked: an attempt to marry 'inappropriate' subject matter to fairly conventional 'pop' song structures. To try and create the kind of pop music I wished had been there for me in my hour of need.

This kind of friction between the words and the music presents problems for me when displaying the lyrics in isolation. Ever since lyric sheets started to be included in my record releases, I have included the instructions, *NB Please do not read the lyrics whilst listening to the recordings*. This is because the words only exist to be part of something else, a song, and when you see them on a printed page you are seeing them taken out of their natural habitat – away from that 'something else'. Sometimes they work with the music, sometimes they work against it but seeing a lyric in print is like watching the TV with the sound turned down: you're only getting half the story. You wouldn't listen to the drums on a track in isolation from all the other instruments that were playing at the same time. I especially don't want people to extract the words from their natural habitat *whilst* the music is actually playing. I remember buying Pink Floyd's *Dark Side of the Moon* as a teenager and rushing home to play it. I sat with the gatefold sleeve open on my knees, poring over Roger Waters' words whilst the album revolved on the record deck – and, to my horror, it made the lyrics seem awful. What had seemed profound and meaningful on the bus ride home from town now seemed clunky and awkward: the syntax mangled and the words crudely shoehorned to fit the rhythm of the music or the vocal melody. Usually when you read something it has the natural tempo of speech, but in a song it has to become subservient to the rhythm of the music it goes with. This concern about how the lyrics were perceived also fed into how they were presented on the lyric sheets. Here is an example from the album *His 'n' Hers*:

> Joyriders. We like driving on a Saturday night, past the Leisure Centre, left at the lights. We don't look for trouble but if it comes we don't run. Looking out for trouble is what we call fun. Hey you, you in the Jesus sandals, wouldn't you like to come over and watch some vandals smashing up someone's home? We can't help it, we're so thick we can't think, can't think of anything but shit, sleep and drink. Oh, and we like women; "up the women" we say and if we get lucky we might even meet some one day. Hey you, you in the Jesus sandals . . . etc. Mister, we just want your car 'cos we're taking a girl to the reservoir. Oh, all the papers say it's a tragedy but don't you want to come and see? Mister we want your car . . . etc. (x 3)

I have always had an extreme aversion to the way lyrics are often typeset to resemble poetry. Lyrics are *not* poetry: they are the words to a song. This obviously presented challenges regarding this collection – a whole book consisting of page after page of text set as above would not be a very pleasant reading experience so, with the help of the publisher, I have attempted to arrive at a form that presents the words in an intelligible manner, designed to work on the page rather than mimic the way they come across in the songs. I guess the success of this approach rather depends on your level of familiarity with the source material but I hope it helps the words to stand up on their own at last. These are still the words to songs but, collected between these covers at least, they are now a written work in their own right. (Definitely *not* poetry though!)

The lyrics are presented in chronological order. I have spared you my very first attempts, dating from 1978, which were either very silly (e.g. 'Shakespeare Rock': *Gotta baby only one thing wrong: she quotes Shakespeare all day long. I said, 'Baby why're you ignoring me?' She said, 'To be or not to be.'*) or embarrassingly earnest (e.g. 'Life is a Circle': *Life is a circle you're caught on. Life is a road that's much too long. It winds, goes ahead – only stops when you're dead.*) So the collection spans the years 1983 to 2009. I've never kept a journal or diary, so the songs are the nearest thing I have to a record of my personal development (or lack of it). If I have learnt anything about songwriting in the interim, it is that in order to ring true it must be rooted in your own personal experience (but not take the place of it). I would subscribe to Leonard Cohen's view, 'Art is just the ash left if your life is burning well.' Life is the important bit and detail is key – as only a true eye-witness would notice apparently insignificant minutiae. When you put such details into songs, they bestow authenticity. I think that you don't really have much control over what does and does not stick in your mind and it's the haphazard nature of memory that gives you an original voice – provided that you can learn to recognise it and use it. Not all the things your brain presents for your consideration are particularly palatable or polite but if they do come to the forefront of your consciousness then they are worth taking notice of. The worst thing you can do is to make a conscious effort to ignore all that stuff and write 'properly', to try to do it 'how it's supposed to be'. That happens a lot – or maybe people don't value their own experience enough to deem it worthy of being written down. It wasn't until I moved away from Sheffield in 1988 that I began to write explicitly about the place – I couldn't really see it clearly until then. Then I wrote about it in a frantic attempt to stop it fading from my memory. I couldn't wait to get away from there, yet then I obsessively recreated it in my mind. Only better. It's good to keep in all the awkward moments and false starts but you *can* mess with the order a bit and adjust the lighting when needs be. You're the boss, after all – it's your kingdom. No one needs to know where reality ends and wishful thinking takes over.

For whatever reason my songs have always been narrative-based. Sometimes I'd love to be able to get away with being allusive and vague but any time I've tried it's been a disaster. You're stuck with what you're capable of doing: a skill is really just a disability in disguise. Sometimes the narrative takes over completely and I dispense with any melody whatsoever and just 'talk' a song. There are examples of this all through the book from 1989's 'My Legendary Girlfriend' to the last lyric included ('You're in My Eyes (Discosong)' from 2009). I probably got the idea of doing this by listening to 'The Gift' by the Velvet Underground or maybe it was Roger McGough's work with The Scaffold. If you can't think of a decent tune to go with the music then don't bother – just speak your way through it. Otherwise you're getting dangerously close to opera (and that's *really* dangerous).

Why *Mother, Brother, Lover*? Well, whilst reading through all the lyrics in order to make this selection I was shocked to find how many times I had used that particular rhyming scheme (there are a few examples in the book but more in some of the songs I have left out). So of course it had to be the title. That's another thing I've learnt over the years: turn your defects into selling points. Don't attempt to hide a fault – exaggerate it. Make it so big that no one can see it any more.

I have included a section of notes in the back of the book which will hopefully shed light on some of the songs' details and also provide some useful background information. They shouldn't be essential to your enjoyment but I hope they may add to it.

*

I began this essay by stating that lyrics aren't really important in pop music but, of course, over the years I have found many exceptions to this rule. Chart pop (what a quaint term) might not provide much linguistic sustenance but once you get off the beaten path it's there to be found. I mentioned Lou Reed and the Velvet Underground earlier but Scott Walker, Leonard Cohen, Lee Hazelwood, Jim Morrison, Dory Previn, David Bowie, Mark E. Smith, Nick Cave, Jeffrey Lewis, Will Oldham and Bill Callahan are just some of the other writers I have admired for their ability to tackle thought-provoking subject matter in song. I thank them for their inspiration. (And let's not forget Dylan – I came to him late but something like 'A Simple Twist of Fate' is a magical example of storytelling in song).

There is a quote from Albert Camus on the back cover of Scott Walker's album *Scott 4*: 'A man's work is nothing but this slow trek to discover, through the detours of art, those two or three great and simple images in whose presence his heart first opened.' That kind of nails it: those images get embedded when you're too young to know much about it and then you spend the rest of your life trying to excavate them. If you're lucky, they're worth the effort.

A recent exhibition of the work of American artist Jeff Koons was called 'Everything's Here'. I wholeheartedly subscribe to that world-view: you *can* live on 'lipgloss and cigarettes'. There are more references to TV shows and showbiz entertainers in these songs than references to the Greek myths but it's all valid. You can mythologise anything if you put your mind to it. In a way it's more fun to look for profundity in something that's not designed to have it. Or maybe that's just awkwardness on my part – I do have a tendency towards that. When I was nine years old, we were learning how to draw bar charts at school and the teacher decided to construct one based on the times we got up in the morning to get ready for school. For some reason I was determined to have a bar on the graph all to myself and so claimed to rise at 6 a.m. every morning (which was an obvious lie as I was usually at least five minutes late each day). The teacher was sceptical but let it go and, much to my satisfaction, I got my own exclusive bar. I don't know why I was so determined to be different from all the other members of my class, but it felt important to me. Perhaps it still is. But I'd like to think that it was more than mere cussedness on my part. That it was the start of a sensibility, a desire to look in the less obvious places – less obvious because they were right under your nose. 'Pulp': the perfect name for it because this was an attempt to find meaning in the mass-produced and throw-away that after all we were surrounded by on a daily basis.

To sift through and find some beauty in it all.

Take a look – it is there.

THE GREAT BARRIER REEF / SHEPHERD'S BUSH
AUGUST 2011

## My Lighthouse

Come up to my lighthouse for I have something I wish to say.
It can wait for a moment, well in fact it can wait all day.
I just wanted to bring you up here so you could have the
chance to see the beauty of the situation that you could share
with me.

It may seem strange to talk of love and then lighthouses,
it's not strange to me.
All alone, you and I in our high tower,
that's the way to be.

Some laugh at my lighthouse, they say that it's just an ivory
tower. But I don't mind because I know their envy grows by
the hour. See, I have a purpose up here: to guide the ships
upon their way. All this is mine; it could be yours too – what
do you say?

It may seem strange to talk of love and then lighthouses – it's
not strange to me.

## Little Girl (with Blue Eyes)

You're just a little girl (with blue eyes). Everybody looks at
you (well, it's your day) and you're stepping from the black
car, but you'll be getting back in soon (and on your way).

Little girl (with blue eyes),
there's a hole in your heart
and one between your legs.
You've never had to wonder
which one he's going to fill
in spite of what he said.
You'll never get away,
hey,
you'll give it up one day,
come what may.

Dad's not got a shotgun, but his look's enough to murder you
(see what you've done), and forget about the paintings 'cos
you'd better get the washing done (oh, something's wrong).

Face down on the pavement, chalk lines round your little
hands (hit and run), and now a mother sits in silence in a
darkness she can't understand (where you've gone). Oh.

Little girl (with blue eyes),
there's a hole in your heart
and one between your legs.
You've never had to wonder
which one he's going to fill.

## 97 Lovers

97 lovers twisted out of shape, and just one kiss could set
them straight.
97 lovers twisted out of shape, and just one kiss could set
them straight.

I know a woman with a picture of Roger Moore in a short
towelling dressing-gown pinned to her bedroom wall. She
married a man who works on a building site. Now they make
love beneath Roger every Friday night.

97 lovers twisted out of shape, and just one kiss could set
them straight.
97 lovers rose to meet the sun, and when the day was over
there were only 91.

Another I know well she laughs too loud with her friends,
playing it safe on the surface to give her heart time to mend.
And then one day without warning he walks unannounced
through the door and he picks her heart up off the table and
he watches it smash on the floor.

Oh, 97 lovers twisted out of shape, and just one kiss could
set them straight.
97 lovers rose to meet the sun, and when the day was over
there were only 91.
(I never found out what happened to the other six.)

## My Legendary Girlfriend

Y'know, sometimes, when we're lying together, and I know
you're asleep (I can hear the soft sound of your breathing).
So I get up and I go to the window. Outside I can see all the
houses – curtains shut tight against the night. Asleep beneath
the roof tiles.

And as I stand there, I wonder,
I wonder how many more times I'm going to come here.
I wonder how many more times I'm going to lie here.
But most of all I wonder what it means.
I just want to know what it means.

So I woke her and we went walking through the sleeping
town, down deserted streets,
frozen gardens grey in the moonlight,
fences,
down to the canal,
creeping slowly past cooling towers,
deserted factories,
looking for an adventure.
I wander the streets calling your name,
jumping walls, hoping to see a light in your window.
Let me in,
let me in tonight.
I see you shivering in the garden,
silver gooseflesh in the moonlight.
She is balancing,
there are so many others with unbroken eyes
and no cellulite afternoons,
she is balancing,
balancing on the edge of ugliness tonight,

she is balancing.
Good God!

My Legendary Girlfriend, she is crying tonight.
Oh no, she doesn't feel right,
she's got no one to hold.
Her love is a sham, he is dancing somewhere.
Oh no, he doesn't care and he'll never know.

Touch me now,
c'mon, c'mon, I don't care, 'cos tonight,
you know, maybe we could touch the sky,
do you think that we could touch the sky?
Please.
I know it's not for ever but tonight I don't care,
your skin so pale in the moonlight,
and the way your lips swell up when you're asleep,
nothing else matters.
Do you know how much I want you?
Can you feel how much I want you?
*Oh, Pitsmoor Woman, oh, let me in tonight!*

My Legendary Girlfriend, she is crying tonight.
Oh no, she doesn't feel right,
she's got no one to hold.
Her love is a sham, he is dancing somewhere.
Oh no, he doesn't care, oh and he'll never know.
And all the stars came out tonight,
and the moon came on his face.
It shone right through the clothes she wore.
It shone right through the dress she wore.

Oh, good God,
oh, listen, listen, please.

I just wanna . . . you don't understand, it's not like that any more, please, please, I just wanna, I just wanna . . . He falls asleep again – no cheese tonight – she knows.

My Legendary Girlfriend, she is crying tonight.
Oh no, she doesn't feel right,
she's got no one to hold.
Her love is a sham, he is dancing somewhere.
Oh no, he doesn't care, oh, and he'll never know.
And oh, the stars came out tonight
and the moon came on his face.
It shone right through the dress she wore.
It shone right through the clothes she wore.
And the sun
and the moon
and the stars
all came down today.
Oh, please love me tonight.

Good God, now.

# Countdown

Oh, I was seventeen when I heard the countdown start. It
started slowly and I thought it was my heart, but then I
realised that this time it was for real: there was no place to
hide – I had to go out and feel, but there was time to kill and
so I walked my way round town. I tried to love the world,
but the world just got me down and so I looked for you in
every street of every town. I want to see your face.

I want to see you now,
I want to see you now.

So it went. So it went for several years. I couldn't stand it – it
must be getting near but you just don't know – no, you just
don't understand how many times I've seen you in the arms
of some other man. I've got to meet you and find you and
take you by the hand. Oh my god, my god, you've got to
understand that I was seventeen. I didn't know a thing at all
– I've got no reason, I've got no reason at all.
Oh no.

Time of my life – I think you came too soon. (Yeah, you came
too soon, babe.)
And it could, it could be tonight if I ever leave this room. (I
never ever leave this room.)
Wasting all my time on all those stupid things that only get
me down. (Get down now.)
And the sky is crying out tonight for me to leave this town,
so I'm going to leave this town.
Bye bye.

You can leave me – you can go some other place – you can

forget it. You know that's okay because I own this town.
Yeah, I brought it to its knees – can't you hear it crying?
Can't you hear it begging to me, 'Please'?
I know it's coming, so soon now – it's on its way
Oh no – I can hear them say –
they say I'll never fly –
they say I'll never leave the ground,
they say it's all a lie and now it's coming down.
Oh, baby, now, please.

Time of my life – I think you came too soon.

It's okay, you don't have to care, really, oh really, I swear.
You owe nothing – you owe nothing to me, and if I mess it
up then that's all up to me. And if you go then I won't follow,
no, though so many times I'll be thinking maybe I should.
No, I'm gonna stay.

I'm gonna make my way,
I'm gonna get on through,
I'm gonna make it some day.

Time of my life – I think you came too soon.

But now the sky is crying out tonight for me to leave this
town, so I'm going to leave this town – really.

Bye bye.

I'm going to leave this town,
I'm not going to hang around.
Leave the ground and fly and never never ever land.
Sun and stars and moon are falling down.

# Space

You said you wanted some space . . . well, is this enough for
you? This is what you've waited for . . . no dust collecting in
corners . . . or cups of tea that go cold before you drink them
. . . Tonight, travelling at the speed of thought, we're gonna
escape into the stars . . . it doesn't matter if the lifts are out
of order . . . or the car won't start . . . we're rising up . . .
above the city . . . above forests . . . and fields . . . rivers and
lakes . . . into the clouds . . . and there up above us the whole
universe is shining in welcome . . .
Did you ever think this day would happen? . . . after days
trying to sell washing machines in the rain . . . it looked like
we'd never leave the ground . . . but we're weightless, floating
free . . . we can go wherever we want . . . solar systems . . .
constellations . . . galaxies . . . I'll race you to the nearest
planet . . .
How many times have you wished upon a star? Now you can
touch one, you can touch the stars, go on, don't be afraid. I
remember you wanted some space . . . well, is this enough for
you? Is it? . . . Oh, the stars are bright . . . but they don't give
out any heat . . . The planets are lumps of rock . . . floating
in a vacuum . . . Yeah, space is cold . . . when you're on your
own . . . I think it's time to go home . . . Pull my string . . .
like a kite that flew too high . . . Now it's time to come down
. . . look out below . . . Wait till I get back . . . You're gonna
see something . . . Yeah, I wanted some space . . . but now
I know . . . It's okay, space is okay . . . But I'd rather . . . I'd
rather get my kicks down below. Oh yeah, c'mon,

Get down.

# Babies

Well, it happened years ago, when you lived on Stanhope
Road. We listened to your sister when you came home from
school 'cos she was two years older and she had boys in her
room. I listened outside, I heard her, alright.

Well, that was alright for a while but soon I wanted more:
I wanted to see as well as hear, so I hid inside her wardrobe
and she came home round four and she was with some kid
called David from the garage up the road. I listened outside,
I heard her, alright.

Oh, I wanna take you home,
I wanna give you children.
You might be my girlfriend.
Yeah.

When I saw you next day I really couldn't tell 'cos you
might go and tell your mother and so you went with Neve
– oh yeah, and Neve was coming on and I thought I heard
you laughing when his mum and dad were gone. I listened
outside, I heard you, alright.

Oh, I wanna take you home,
I wanna give you children.
You might be my girlfriend.
Yeah.

Oh yeah.

Oh well, I guess it couldn't last too long: I came home one
day and all her things were gone. I fell asleep inside – I never

heard her come and then she opened up the wardrobe and I
had to . . . get it on.

Oh, listen:

We were on the bed when you came home.
I heard you stop outside the door.
I know you won't believe it's true:
I only went with her 'cos she looks like you.
My god!

Oh, I wanna take you home,
I wanna give you children.
You might be my girlfriend.
Yeah.

Oh yeah.

# Sheffield: Sex City

Intake . . . Manor Park . . . The Wicker . . . Norton . . .
Frechville . . . Hackenthorpe . . . Shalesmoor . . .
Wombwell . . . Catcliffe . . . Brincliffe . . . Attercliffe . . .
Ecclesall . . . Woodhouse . . . Wybourn . . . Pitsmoor . . .
Badger . . . Wincobank . . . Crookes . . . Walkley . . .
Broomhill

CANDIDA: *I was only about eleven when this happened. We
were living in a big block of flats with a central courtyard. All
the bedroom windows in the building opened onto this court,
and sometimes in the middle of the night, in that building it
sounded like a mass orgy. I may have been only eleven, but
no one had to tell me what all that moaning and yelling was
about. I'd lie there mesmerised, listening to the first couple.
Invariably, they'd wake up other couples, and like some kind
of chain reaction, within minutes the whole building was
fucking. I mean, have you ever heard other people fucking
and really enjoying it? It's a marvellous sound. Not like in the
movies, but when it's real. It's such a happy, exciting sound.*

The city is a woman bigger than any other.
Oh, sophisticated lady,
I wanna be your lover,
not your brother or your mother, yeah.

The sun rose from behind the gasometers at 6.30 a.m., crept
through the gap in your curtains and caressed your bare feet
poking from beneath the floral sheets. I watched him flaking
bits of varnish from your nails trying to work his way up
under the sheets.

[ 20 ]

Jesus! Even the sun's on heat today, the whole city getting
stiff in the building heat.
I just want to make contact with you,
oh, that's all I wanna do.
I just want to make contact with you,
oh, that's all I wanna do.

Now I'm trying hard to meet her
but the fares went up at seven.
She is somewhere in the city,
somewhere watching television.
Watching people being stupid,
doing things she can't believe in.
Love won't last till the next instalment,
ten o'clock on Tuesday evening.

And the world is going on outside.
The night is gaping open wide.
The wardrobe and the chest of drawers
are telling her to go outdoors.
He should have been here by this time,
he said that he'd be here by nine.
That guy is such a prick sometimes.
I don't know why you bother really.

Oh, babe, oh, I'm sorry,
but I just had to make love to every crack in the pavement
and the shop doorways
and the puddles of rain that reflected your face in my eyes.

The day didn't go too well, too many chocolates and
cigarettes, I kept thinking of you and almost walking into
lamp posts. Why is it so hot? The air coming to the boil,
rubbing up against walls and lamp posts trying to get rid of it.

Old women clack their tongues in the shade of crumbling
concrete bus shelters.
Dogs doing it, in central reservations, and causing multiple
pile-ups in the centre of town.

I didn't want to go in the first place but I've been sentenced
to three years in the housing-benefit waiting room.

I must have lost your number in the all-night garage and now
I'm wandering up and down your street calling your name.
In the rain.
Whilst my shoes turn to sodden cardboard.

JARVIS: Where are you?
                          CANDIDA: I'm here.
JARVIS: Where are you?
                          CANDIDA: I'm here.
JARVIS: Where are you?
                          CANDIDA: I'm here.
JARVIS: Where are you?
                          CANDIDA: I'm here.
JARVIS: Where are you?
                          CANDIDA: I'm here.
JARVIS: Where are you? . . .

I'm still trying hard to meet you
but it doesn't look like happening
'cos the city's out to get me,
but I won't sleep with her this evening.
Though her buildings are impressive
and her cul-de-sacs amazing,
she's had too many lovers
and I know you're out there waiting.

And now she's getting into bed,
he's had his chance, now it's too late.
The carpets screaming for her soul,
the darkness wants to eat her whole.
Tonight must be the night it ends.
Tomorrow she will call her friends
and go out on her own somewhere.
Who needs this shit anyway?

Oh, listen. I wandered the streets the whole night
trying to pick up your scent,
writing messages on walls.
And the puddles of rain reflected your face in my eyes.

We finally made it . . .

On a hilltop at 4 a.m.
the whole city is your jewellery box.
A million twinkling yellow street lights.
Reach out and take what you want.
You can have it all.
Jesus, it took a long time.
I didn't think we were going to make it.
So bad during the day,
but now snug and warm under an eiderdown sky.

*All the Things We Saw:*

Everyone on Park Hill came in unison at 4.13 a.m.
and the whole block fell down.

The tobacconist caught fire
and everyone in the street died of lung cancer.

We heard groans from a T-reg Chevette:

You bet,
you bet, yeah.

Oh, I was trying hard to meet her
but the fares went up at seven.
She was somewhere in the city,
somewhere watching television.
Watching people being stupid,
doing things she can't believe in.
Love won't last till next instalment,
ten o'clock on Tuesday evening.
Oh, the world was going on outside.
The night was gaping open wide.
The wardrobe and the chest of drawers
were telling her to go outdoors.
He should have been there by that time,
he said that he'd be there by nine.
The guy is such a prick sometimes, yeah.

Oh, babe, I wanna . . . I wanna to tell you that there's
nothing . . . nothing to worry about because we can . . . get it
together. Oh yeah. Oh . . . we got it together tonight . . .

Didn't we?

# Razzmatazz

The trouble with your brother?
He's always sleeping with your mother and I know that your
sister missed her time again this month.
Am I talking too fast or are you just playing dumb?
If you want I can write it down.
It shouldn't matter to you 'cos aren't you the one with your
razzmatazz and the nights on the town?

Oh, you knew it and you blew it, didn't you, babe?
I was lying when I asked you to stay.

And now no one's going to care if you don't call when you said.
And he's not coming round tonight to try and talk you into
bed. And all those stupid little things, they ain't working.
No, they ain't working any more.

You started getting fatter three weeks after I left you
and now you're going with some kid who looks like some
bad comedian.
Are you going to go out or are you staying at home eating
boxes of Milk Tray?
Watch TV on your own – oh, aren't you the one?
With your razzmatazz and the nights on the town.

And your father wants to help you, doesn't he, babe?
But your mother wants to put you away.

And now no one's going to care if you don't call when you
said. And he's not coming round tonight to try and talk you
into bed. And all those stupid little things, they ain't working.
No, they ain't working any more.

Oh well, I saw you at the doctor's waiting for a test.
You're trying to look like some kind of heiress but your face
is such a mess and now you're going to a party and leaving
on your own.
Oh, I'm sorry, but didn't you say, 'Things go better with a
little bit of razzmatazz'?

Now no one's going to care if you don't call when you said.

# Inside Susan: A Story in Three Songs

## 1 *Stacks*

I saw you standing at the stop in your crochet halter top and
your sky-blue trainer bra. I know you're gonna go too far.
You're driving all the boys insane down by the sports hall in
the rain. Chewing gum and navy dress, purple shirt and all
the rest.
There's stacks to do and there's stacks to see and there's stacks
to touch and there's stacks to be. So many ways for you to
spend your time. Such a lot but I know that you've got . . .

I heard you let him touch too much on the back seat of the
bus. Did you stay over at his place? And did you do it? Was
he ace? The world is bigger every day and you've always got
something to say and you've always got somewhere to go.
Oh, it's getting faster, don't you know?
And there's stacks to do and there's stacks to see. And there's
stacks to touch and there's stacks to be. So many ways for
you to spend your time. Such a lot. But I know that you've
got . . .

Places to go and faces to kiss and boys to confuse and
appointments to miss. So many ways for you to spend your
time. Such a lot. Yes, I know that you've got . . .
You've got stacks.

## 2 *Inside Susan*

Susan catches the bus into town at 10.30 a.m. and sits on the
back seat. She looks at the man in front's head and thinks
how his fat, wrinkled neck looks like a large carrot sticking

out from the collar of his shirt. She adds up the numbers on her bus ticket to see if they make twenty-one – but they don't. Maybe she shouldn't bother going to school at all then. Her friends will be in the yard with their arms folded on their chests, pushing up their breasts to try and make them look bigger, while the boys will be too busy playing football to notice.

The bus is waiting on the high street when it suddenly begins to rain torrentially and it sounds like someone has emptied about a million packets of dried peas onto the roof of the bus. 'What if it just keeps raining?' she thinks to herself. 'And it was just like being in an aquarium except it was all shoppers and office workers that were floating past the windows instead of fish.' She's still thinking about this as the bus goes past Caroline Lee's house, where there was a party last week. There were some German exchange students over who were very immature. They ended up jumping out of the bedroom window. One of them tried to get her to kiss him on the stairs – so she kicked him. Later she was sick because she'd drunk too much cider. Caroline was drunk as well, she was pretending that she was married to a tall boy in glasses, and she had to wear a polo neck for three days afterwards to cover up the love bite on her neck.

By now the bus is going past the markets. Outside is a man who spends all day forcing felt-tip pens into people's hands and then trying to make them pay for them. She used to work in a pet shop there, but she got sacked for talking to boys when she was supposed to be working. She wasn't too bothered though: she hated the smell of the rabbits anyway.

'Maybe this bus won't stop,' she thinks, 'and I'll stay on it until I'm old enough to go into pubs on my own, and it'll drive me to a town where people with black hair are treated

specially, and I can make lots of money from charging fat old
men five pounds a time to look up my skirt, and they'll be
queuing up to take me out to dinner.'

I suppose you think she's just a silly girl with stupid ideas,
but I remember her in those days. They talk about people
with a fire within and all that stuff. Well, she had that alright
– it's just that nobody dared to jump into her fire and risk
being consumed. Instead they put her in a corner and let her
heat up the room, warming their hands and backsides in
front of her, and then slagging her off around town.

No one ever really got inside Susan, and she always ended up
getting off the bus at the terminus and then walking home.

## 3 59, *Lyndhurst Grove*

There's a picture by his first wife on the wall,
stripped floorboards in the kitchen and the hall,
a stain from last week's party on the stairs,
but no one knows who made it, or how it ever got there.
They were dancing with children round their necks,
talking business, books and records, art and sex.
All things being considered, you'd call it a success.
You wore your black dress.
Oh.
He's an architect and such a lovely guy,
and he'll stay with you until the day you die.
And he'll give you everything you could desire.
Oh well – almost everything: everything that he can buy.
So you sometimes go out in the afternoon,
spend an hour with your lover in his bedroom,
hearing old women rolling trolleys down the road
back to Lyndhurst Grove.
Lyndhurst Grove.

# The Babysitter

Susan's babysitter is seventeen years old,
she looks like Susan when she still lived at home.
She's a lovely girl,
she's got long black hair.
If you go home now she might still be there.

Susan's babysitter is twenty-one years old,
she still looks like Susan but Susan's not at home.
She's a lonely girl,
she's got permed long hair.
If you go home now she will not be there
'cos she left last June.
She came home too soon,
you were both upstairs in your daughter's room.

She's a lonely girl.

# Lipgloss

No wonder you're looking thin when all that you live on is
lipgloss and cigarettes and scraps at the end of the day, when
he's given the rest to someone with long black hair.
All those nights in, making such a mess of the bed, you never,
ever want to go home and he wants you, so you may as well
hang around for a while.
Call your dad on the phone.

He changed his mind last Monday, so you've got to leave by
Sunday.
Yeah.

Oh, you've lost your lipgloss, honey.
Oh yeah, now nothing you do can turn him on.
There's something wrong.
You had it once but now it's gone.

And you feel such a fool for laughing at bad jokes and
putting up with all of his friends and kissing in public.
What are they gonna say when they run into you again?
That your stomach looks bigger and your hair is a mess and
your eyes are just holes in your face.
And it rains every day and when it doesn't, the sun makes
you feel worse anyway.

He changed his mind last Monday, so you've got to leave by
Sunday.
Yeah, you've lost your lipgloss, honey.
Now nothing you do can turn him on.
There's something wrong.
You had it once but now it's gone.

Though you knew there was no way it was going to last for ever, it still shook you when he told you in a letter that he didn't want to see you. You nearly lost your mind.

Now you've lost your lipgloss, honey.

## Street Lites

Doorways
Corners
And the street lights dance in your eyes.
Behind the cinema,
in the rain,
in the subway where the walls crumble and cover you in fine
dust.
'Cos we haven't got a home to go to.
Touch me by the railings,
on the back seat
or the top deck
or the back row.
Can you feel me against you?
Oh, you know we shouldn't – but I want to.

What you gonna do if you go home and he's not there?
It wouldn't be the same if we didn't know it was wrong.
Touch me and then go whilst I can still taste you.
Yeah, leave me and I'll walk it off in the rain somehow.

Someone wants to watch by the side of the Lina Stores.
Policewoman chasing newspapers.
Hiding in doorways.
Did they see us?
And do you care?
Pull the night-time tight around us and we can keep each
other warm whilst cars drive by en route to dried-up dinners
in strip-lit kitchens and the smell of gas and potato peelings.

What you gonna do if you go home and he's not there?
It wouldn't be the same if we didn't know it was wrong.

Touch me and then go whilst I can still taste you.
Yeah, leave me and I'll walk it off in the rain somehow.

*Walking, walking, . . .*

We've got to go on meeting like this. I don't want to live with you or anywhere near you.
I want to catch you unawares,
undressing in front of a window.
Maybe even pressing up next to him as I drive by.
Did you see me?
Could you tell that I was watching?
Did it make it feel better?
Yeah, it was good for me too.
Did you think about me?
Did you close your eyes and think that maybe it was my hand that was touching you?
My breath against your face?
And when you opened your eyes did the world tip off its axis for a few seconds?
And you thought you caught a tiny glimpse of something hidden behind his shoulder as he moved towards you?
Yeah, I felt it too –
and it felt good.
It felt good in the strange kind of way:
in the way that things that aren't *supposed* to feel good sometimes do.

What you gonna do if you go home and he's not there?
It wouldn't be the same if we didn't know it was wrong.

# Do You Remember the First Time?

You say you've got to go home 'cos he's sitting on his own
again this evening and I know you're gonna let him bore
your pants off again.
Oh, now it's half past eight –
you'll be late.

But you say you're not sure:
though it makes good sense for you to live together,
still you bought a toy that can reach the places he never goes.
And now it's getting late.
He's so straight.

Do you remember the first time?
I can't remember a worse time, but you know that we've
changed so much since then:
oh yeah, we've grown.
Now I don't care what you're doing,
no, I don't care if you screw him,
just as long as you save a piece for me.
Oh yeah now.

You wanna go home.
Well, at least there's someone there that you can talk to and
you never have to face up to the night on your own.
Jesus, it must be great to be straight.

Do you remember the first time?
I can't remember a worse time, but you know that we've
changed so much since then:
oh yeah, we've grown.
Now I don't care what you're doing,

no, I don't care if you screw him,
just as long as you save a piece for me.
Oh yeah now.

You say you've got to go home.

# Deep-Fried in Kelvin

Oh, children of the future – conceived in the toilets of
Meadowhall – to be raised on cheap corn snacks and garage
food. Rolling empty cans down the stairwell. Don't you love
that sound? Like the thoughts of a bad social worker rattling
around his head . . . Trying to remember what he learned at
training college . . . 'Mester said you wasn't allowed in here –
so why don't you get lost?'

And if you're good then when you grow up maybe you can
live on Kelvin. Yeah, you can live in Kelvin. And promenade
the concrete walkways where pigeons go to die.

*A woman on the fourteenth floor noticed that her ceiling
was bulging as if under a great weight. When the council
investigated they discovered that the man in the flat above
had transported a large quantity of soil into his living room,
in which several plants he had stolen from the local park
were growing. When questioned, the man said that all he had
wanted was a garden.*

Oh God, I think the future has been deep-fried – deep-fried
in Kelvin. And now it's rotting behind the remains of a stolen
motorbike. 'I never touched it, honest, but there was nothing
else to do.'

We don't need your sad attempts at social conscience based
on taxi rides home at night from exhibition openings. We just
want your car radio and bass-reflex speakers.
Now.

Suffer the little children to come unto me, and I will tend

their adventure-playground splinters and cigarette burns, and
feed them fizzy orange and chips – that they may grow up
straight and tall. That they may grow up to live on Kelvin.
Oh yeah, we can have ghettos too, only we use air rifles
instead of machine guns – stitch that.
And we drink Diamond White.

In the end, the question you have to ask yourself is:
are you talking to me,
or are you chewing a brick?

# Joyriders

We like driving on a Saturday night
past the leisure centre, left at the lights.
We don't look for trouble
but if it comes we don't run.
Looking out for trouble is what we call fun.

Hey you –
you in the Jesus sandals –
wouldn't you like to come over and watch some vandals
smashing up someone's home?

We can't help it, we're so thick we can't think.
Can't think of anything but shit, sleep and drink.
Oh, and we like women –
'Up the women,' we say,
and if we get lucky we might even meet some one day.

Hey you –
you in the Jesus sandals –
wouldn't you like to come over and watch some vandals
smashing up someone's home?

Mister, we just want your car 'cos we're taking a girl to the
reservoir.
Oh, all the papers say it's a tragedy.

But don't you want to come and see?

Mister, we just want your car 'cos we're taking a girl to the
reservoir.
Oh, all the papers say it's a tragedy.

## Acrylic Afternoons

I fell asleep on your sofa and I had a dream about a small
child in dungarees who caught his hands in the doors of the
Paris metro. Then my face cracked open and you were there.
You were there dressed in green, saying something obscene,
but that's why I came here in the first place.
Oh well, that and the tea.

Can I stay here lying under the table together with you now?
Can I hold you? For ever in acrylic afternoons.
I want to hold you tight whilst children play outside
and they wait for their mothers to finish with lovers and call
them inside for their tea.

Cushions and TV and the table's set for tea. One for you,
one for me. Come and lie down on the settee. In that green
jumper you can have anything you want, and the clock is
saying that it's half past four but you know I want to stay a
little more.
I want to stay a little more.

Can I stay here lying under the table together with you now?
Can I hold you? For ever in acrylic afternoons.
I want to hold you tight whilst children play outside
and they wait for their mothers to finish with lovers and call
them inside for their tea.

On a pink quilted eiderdown I want to pull your knickers
down.

Net curtains blowing slightly in the breeze,
Lemonade light filtering through the trees.

It's so soft and it's warm. Just another cup of tea, please.
One lump, yeah – thank you.

Can I stay here lying under the table together with you now?
Can I hold you? For ever in acrylic afternoons.
I want to hold you tight whilst children play outside
and they wait for their mothers to finish with lovers and call
them inside for their tea.

Oh, Wayne, Julie, Diane, Kevin, Shane, Heather, Rachel,
Chelsea, Leanne – come home.
Your mum misses you.

# David's Last Summer

We made our way slowly down the path that led to the stream, swaying slightly, drunk on the sun, I suppose. It was a real summer's day. The air humming with heat, whilst the trees beckoned us into their cool green shade. And when we reached the stream, I put a bottle of cider into the water to chill, both of us knowing that we'd drink it long before it had chance.

This is where you want to be, there's nothing else but you and her and how you spend your time.

Walking to parties whilst it's still light outside. Peter was upset at first but now he's in the garden talking to somebody Polish. Why don't we set up a tent and spend the night out there? And we can pretend that we're somewhere foreign but we'll still be able to use the fridge if we get hungry or too hot.

This is where you want to be, there's nothing else but you and her and how you use your time.
We went driving.

The room smells faintly of suntan lotion in the evening sunlight and when you take off your clothes you're still wearing a small pale skin bikini. The sound of children playing in the park comes from far away and time slows down to the speed of the specks of dust floating in the light from the window.

Summer leaves fall from summer trees. Summer grazes fade on summer knees. Summer nights are slowly getting long. Summer's going, so hurry, soon it'll be gone.

So we went out to the park at midnight one last time. Past the abandoned glasshouse stuffed full of dying palms. Past the bandstand and down to the boating lake. And we swam in the moonlight for what seemed like hours, until we couldn't swim any more.

And as we came out of the water we both sensed a certain movement in the air and we both shivered slightly and ran to collect our clothes. And as we walked home we could hear the leaves curling and turning brown on the trees, and the birds deciding where to go for the winter. And the whole sound of summer packing its bags and preparing to leave town.

Oh, but I want you to stay.
Oh, please stay for a while.
I don't want to live in the cold.

## His 'n' Hers

I've got the time and you've got the space,
I want to wipe you down and lick the smile off your face,
the smile off your face.
Though we know that it's wrong:
towel sets, matching combs.
Oh, it looks so good but does it turn you on?

I want you now,
I want you here.
So lie down by the fire
and if the neighbours hear,
the neighbours hear,
'cos they don't understand what you've got in your hand.
Oh, it looks so good but does it turn you on?

Are we going to do it again?
Sideways.
I was stood in the queue, then you came,
delivered me from His 'n' Hers.
You pulled the units down,
delivered me from His 'n' Hers.
And when I saw his face it made me feel better.

You've gone too far.
You gave up hope
and the future's bleak.
It's just a soap on a rope.
A soap on a rope.
Put the rope around his neck,
pull it tight:
he's erect

and it looks so good, but does it turn you on?

Are we going to do it again?
Shove it in sideways.
I was stood in the queue, then you came,
delivered me from His 'n' Hers.
You pulled the units down,
delivered me from His 'n' Hers.
And when I saw his face it made me feel better.

So we were laid in bed afterwards and she asked me what
made me frightened and I said:

'I'm frightened of Belgian chocolates
I'm frightened of potpourri,
I'm frightened of James Dean posters,
I'm frightened of 26-inch screens,
I'm frightened of remote control,
I'm frightened of endowment plans,
I'm frightened of figurines,
I'm frightened of evenings in the Brincliffe Oaks searching for
a conversation . . .'

'Oh, you're stupid,' she said, and she took my hand.
She took my hand and she said:

'I want . . .
I want you . . .
I want you to . . .
I want you to touch . . .
I want you to touch me,
I want you to touch me there . . .'

Are we going to do it again?

# Common People

She came from Greece, she had a thirst for knowledge.
She studied sculpture at St Martin's College: that's where I
caught her eye.
She told me that her dad was loaded.
I said, 'In that case I'll have a rum and Coca-Cola.'
She said, 'Fine' – and then in thirty seconds' time she said:
'I want to live like common people,
I want to do whatever common people do,
I want to sleep with common people,
I want to sleep with common people like you.'
Well, what else could I do?
I said, 'I'll see what I can do.'

I took her to a supermarket.
I don't know why, but I had to start it somewhere: so it
started *there*.
I said, 'Pretend you've got no money.'
She just laughed and said, 'Oh, you're so funny.' I said,
'Yeah? Well, I can't see anyone else smiling in here – are you
sure you want to live like common people?
You want to see whatever common people see?
You want to sleep with common people?
You want to sleep with common people like me?'
But she didn't understand –
And she just smiled and held my hand.

Rent a flat above a shop.
Cut your hair and get a job.
Smoke some fags and play some pool.
Pretend you never went to school.
But still you'll never get it right

'cos when you're laid in bed at night watching roaches climb
the wall,
if you called your dad he could stop it all.

You'll never live like common people,
you'll never do what common people do,
you'll never fail like common people,
you'll never watch your life slide out of view
and then dance
and drink
and screw
because there's nothing else to do.

Oh.

Sing along with the common people,
sing along and it might just get you through.
Laugh along with the common people,
laugh along even though they're laughing at you
and the stupid things that you do because you think that
poor is cool.

Like a dog lying in the corner
they will bite you and never warn you: look out,
they'll tear your insides out
'cos everybody hates a tourist.
Especially one who thinks it's all such a laugh,
and the chip stains and grease will come out in the bath.

You will never understand how it feels to live your life
with no meaning or control
and with nowhere left to go.
You are amazed that they exist,
and they burn so bright whilst you can only wonder why.

Rent a flat above a shop.
Cut your hair and get a job.
Smoke some fags and play some pool.
Pretend you never went to school.
Still you'll never get it right
'cos when you're laying in bed at night watching roaches
climb the wall,
if you called your dad he could stop it all, yeah.

You'll never live like common people,
you'll never do what common people do,
you'll never fail like common people,
you'll never watch your life slide out of view
and then dance
and drink
and screw
because there's nothing else to do.

I wanna live with common people like you.

## Sorted for E's & Wizz

Oh, is this the way they say the future's meant to feel? Or
just 20,000 people standing in a field? And I don't quite
understand just what this feeling is, but that's okay 'cos we're
all sorted out for E's and wizz.
And tell me when the spaceship lands 'cos all this has just got
to mean something.

In the middle of the night, it feels alright, but then tomorrow
morning . . . oh, then you come down.

Oh yeah, the pirate radio told us what was going down. Got
the tickets from some fucked-up bloke in Camden Town, and
no one seems to know exactly where it is, but that's okay 'cos
we're all sorted out for E's and wizz.
At four o'clock the normal world seems very, very, very far
away.

In the middle of the night, it feels alright. But then tomorrow
morning . . . oh, then you come down.

Just keep on moving.

Everybody asks your name – they say we're all the same and
now it's 'nice one', 'geezer' – that's as far as the conversation
went. I lost my friends, I dance alone. It's six o'clock, I
wanna go home but it's 'no way', 'not today' – makes you
wonder what it meant. And this hollow feeling grows and
grows and grows and grows, and you want to call your
mother and say, 'Mother, I can never come home again 'cos I
seem to have left an important part of my brain somewhere
in a field in Hampshire.'

Alright.

In the middle of the night, it feels alright, but then tomorrow
morning . . . oh, then you come down.
Oh, then you come down.
What if you never come down?

# Mis-Shapes

Mis-shapes,
mistakes,
misfits,
raised on a diet of broken biscuits.
We don't look the same as you and we don't do the things you
do
but we live around here too,
oh really.

Mis-shapes,
mistakes,
misfits –
we'd like to go to town but we can't risk it 'cos they just want
to keep us out.
You could end up with a smack in the mouth
just for standing out,
now really.

Brothers, sisters, can't you see?
The future's owned by you and me.
There won't be fighting in the street.
They think they've got us beat  but revenge is going to be so
. . . sweet

We're making a move,
we're making it now.
We're coming out of the sidelines.
Just put your hands up: it's a raid.
We want your homes,
we want your lives,
we want the things you won't allow us.

We won't use guns,
we won't use bombs,
we'll use the one thing we've got more of –
that's our minds.

Check your lucky numbers.
That much money could drag you under.
What's the point in being rich if you can't think what to do
with it 'cos you're so bleeding thick?

We weren't supposed to be – we learnt too much at school,
now we can't help but see that the future that you've got
mapped out is nothing much to shout about.

We're making a move,
we're making it now.
We're coming out of the sidelines.
Just put your hands up, it's a raid.
We want your homes,
we want your lives,
we want the things you won't allow us.
We won't use guns,
we won't use bombs,
we'll use the one thing we've got more of –
that's our minds.

We're making a move.

# I Spy

I spy a boy,
I spy a girl.
I spy the worst place in the world,
in the whole wide world.

Oh, you didn't do bad:
you made it out.
I'm still stuck here but I'll get out.

Oh yeah, I'll get out.

Can't you see a giant walks among you,
seeing through your petty lives?
Do you think I do these things for real?
I do these things just so I survive.
And you know I will survive.

It may look to the untrained eye
that I'm sitting on my arse all day –
I'm biding time until the day I take you all on.
My Lords and Ladies,
I shall prevail,
I cannot fail.
'Cos I spy.

Oh, I've got your numbers, taken notes,
I know the ways your minds work;
I have studied.
And your minds are just the same as mine
except that you are clever swines,
you never let your masks slip,

you never admit to it,
you're never hurried.
Oh no, no, no.
And every night I hone my plan
how I will get my satisfaction,
how I will blow your paradise away.
Away,
away,
'cos I spy.

Yeah, it's just like in the old days. I used to compose my
own critical notices in my head: 'The crowd gasp at Cocker's
masterful control of the bicycle, skilfully avoiding the dog
turd outside the corner shop.' Imagining a blue plaque above
the place I first ever touched a girl's chest, but hold on:
you've got to wait for the best.

You see, you should take me seriously. Very seriously indeed.
Because I've been sleeping with your wife for the past sixteen
weeks, smoking your cigarettes, drinking your brandy,
messing up the bed that you chose together – and in all that
time I just wanted you to come home unexpectedly one
afternoon and catch us at it in the front room.

You see, I spy for a living and I specialise in revenge – on
taking the things I know will cause you pain. I can't help it:
I was dragged up. My favourite parks are car parks. Grass is
something you smoke. Birds are something you shag. Take
your *Year in Provence* and shove it up your ass.

Your Ladbroke Grove looks turn me on, yeah.
With roach burns in designer dresses,
skin stretched tight over high cheekbones,
and thousands of tiny dryness lines
beating a path to the corners of your eyes.

And every night I hatch my plan,
it's not a case of 'woman v. man'.
It's more a case of 'haves against haven'ts'.
And I just happen to have got what you need,
just exactly what you need,
yeah.

La la la . . .
in the midnight hour.
La la la . . .
I will come to you,
I will take you from this sickness,
dinner parties and champagne,
I'll hold your body and make it sing again.
Come on – sing again,
let's sing again,
oh yeah,
'cos I spy,
yes, I spy.

I spy a boy,
I spy a girl.
I spy a chance to change the world, to change your world.

# F.E.E.L.I.N.G.C.A.L.L.E.D.L.O.V.E.

The room is cold and has been like this for several months. If
I close my eyes I can visualise everything in it, right down to
the broken handle on the third drawer down of the dressing
table. And the world outside this room has also assumed
a familiar shape – the same events shuffled in a slightly
different order every day. Just like a modern shopping centre.
And it's so cold. Yeah, it's so cold.
What . . . is . . . this . . . feeling called love?
Why me? Why you? Why here? Why now?
It doesn't make no sense, it's not convenient, it doesn't fit my
plans, it's something I don't understand,
F.E.E.L.I.N.G. C.A. double L.E.D. L.O.V.E.
What is this thing that is happening to me?
*(And as I stand and cross the room I feel as if my whole life
has been leading to this one moment. And as I touch your
shoulder tonight this room has become the centre of the
entire universe.)*

So what do I do? I've got a slightly sick feeling in my
stomach, like I'm standing on top of a very high building.
Oh yeah – all the stuff they tell you about in the movies, but
this isn't chocolate boxes and roses. It's dirtier than that –
like some small animal that only comes out at night. And
I see flashes of the shape of your breasts and the curve of
your belly and they make me have to sit down and catch my
breath. And it's so cold. Yeah, it's so cold.
What . . . is . . . this . . . feeling called love?
Why me? Why you? Why here? Why now?
It doesn't make no sense, no, it's not convenient, no, it
doesn't fit my plans. But I've got that taste in my mouth
again, oh.

F.E.E.L.I.N.G. C.A. double L.E.D. L.O.V.E.
What is this thing that is happening to me?
*(And the whole world begins to spin and spin outside the*
*window, faster and faster and faster, and this is the only place*
*in focus, the hook upon which everything else revolves.)*
What is this thing that is happening to me?

# Disco 2000

Oh, we were born within one hour of each other.
Our mothers said we could be sister and brother.
Your name is Deborah.
Deborah,
it never suited you.

And they said that when we grew up we'd get married and
never split up.
Oh, we never did it,
although I often thought of it.

Oh, Deborah, do you recall?
Your house was very small
with woodchip on the wall.
When I came round to call, you didn't notice me at all.

And I said, 'Let's all meet up in the year 2000
Won't it be strange when we're all fully grown?
Be there two o'clock by the fountain down the road.'
I never knew that you'd get married,
I would be living down here on my own,
on that damp and lonely Thursday years ago.

You were the first girl at school to get breasts,
and Martyn said that you were the best.
The boys all loved you but I was a mess.
I had to watch them try and get you undressed.
We were friends, that was as far as it went.
I used to walk you home sometimes but it meant nothing to
you 'cos you were so popular.
Deborah, do you recall?

Your house was very small
with woodchip on the wall.
When I came round to call, you didn't notice me at all.

And I said, 'Let's all meet up in the year 2000
Won't it be strange when we're all fully grown?
Be there at two o'clock by the fountain down the road.'
I never knew that you'd get married,
I would be living down here on my own,
on that damp and lonely Thursday years ago.

Do it,
oh yeah.

Deborah, do you recall?

What are you doing Sunday, baby?
Would you like to come and meet me maybe?
You can even bring your baby.
Oh.

## Something Changed

I wrote this song two hours before we met.
I didn't know your name or what you looked like yet.
I could have stayed at home and gone to bed.
I could have gone to see a film instead.
You might have changed your mind and seen your friend.
Life could have been very different but then:
Something changed.

Do you believe that there's someone up above?
And does he have a timetable directing acts of love?
Why did I write this song on that one day?
Why did you touch my hand and softly say,
'Stop asking questions that don't matter anyway.
Just give us a kiss to celebrate here today:
Something changed.'

When we woke up that morning
we had no way of knowing
that in a matter of hours we'd change the way we were going.
Where would I be now?
Where would I be now if we'd never met?
Would I be singing this song to someone else instead?
I don't know, but like you said:
Something changed.

# Live Bed Show

She doesn't have to go to work but she doesn't want to
stay in bed 'cos it's changed from something comfortable to
something else instead.

This bed has seen it all – from the first time to the last.
The silences of now and the good times of the past.
And it only cost ten pounds from a shop just down the road.
Mind you, that was seven years ago and things were very
different then.

It didn't get much rest at first, the headboard banging in the
night. The neighbours didn't dare complain, everything was
going right.

Now there's no need to complain 'cos it never makes a
sound.
Something beautiful left town and she doesn't even know its
name.

Now every night she plays a sad game called
'Pretending Nothing's Going Wrong'.
Oh, but she knows if this show was televised
no one would watch it.
Not tonight –
but seven years ago . . .

Now there's no need to complain 'cos it never makes a
sound.
Something beautiful left town and she never even knew its
name.

She doesn't have to go to work but doesn't want to stay in bed 'cos it's changed from something comfortable to something else instead.

# Bar Italia

Now if you can stand I would like to take you by the hand,
and go for a walk past people as they go to work.
Let's get out of this place before they tell us that we've just died.

Oh, move, move quick, you've got to move.
Come on, it's through, come on, it's time.
Oh, look at you – you're looking so confused.
Just what did you lose? Oh.

If you can make an order, could you get me one?
Two sugars would be great 'cos I'm fading fast and it's nearly
dawn.
If they knocked down this place, it'd still look much better than
you.

Oh now, move, move quick, you've got to move.
Come on, it's through, come on, it's time.
Oh, look at you – you're looking so confused.
Oh, what did you lose?
Oh, it's okay – it's just your mind.

If we get through this alive, I'll meet you next week, same place,
same time.

That's what you get from clubbing it:
you can't go home and go to bed because it hasn't worn off yet and
now it's morning.
There's only one place we can go.
It's around the corner in Soho,
where other broken people go.

Let's go.

## Mile End

We didn't have nowhere to live,
we didn't have nowhere to go,
till someone said, 'I know this place off Burdett Road.'
It was on the fifteenth floor,
it had a board across the door.
It took an hour to prise it off and get inside.
It smelt as if someone had died.
The living room was full of flies,
the kitchen sink was blocked,
the bathroom sink not there at all.
Oh, it's a mess alright.
Yes, it's Mile End.

And now we're living in the sky.
I never thought I'd live so high.
Just like heaven if it didn't look like hell.
The lift is always full of piss,
the fifth-floor landing smells of fish,
not just on Friday – every single other day.
Below, the kids come out at night,
they kick a ball and have a fight and maybe shoot somebody
if they lose at pool.
Oh, it's a mess alright.
Yes, it's Mile End.

Nobody wants to be your friend
'cos you're not from round here.
As if that was something to be proud about.
The pearly king of the Isle of Dogs
feels up children in the bogs.
Down by the playing fields someone sets a car on fire.

I guess you have to go right down before you understand just how low,
how low a human being can go.
Oh, it's a mess alright.
Yes, it's Mile End.
Mile End.

## Catcliffe Shakedown

Straight down the Parkway, follow your nose to a place
where nobody wants to go. It's a fare and a half; they're
having a larf. Everybody's broken or they're a dwarf.
Pierrot mirror on the wall, who is the ace-est of them all? The
Catcliffe girl who gets out before her eighteenth birthday.
There's a little old man by the side of the road, just where he
came from nobody knows. He's so picturesque, a physical
wreck, a dirty old bloke with no self-respect. Ow!

Oh God! You'd better leave town before you get caught in
the Catcliffe Shakedown. Yeah.

It's a step to the left, a step to the right: you do the Catcliffe
Shakedown with all of your might – oh, baby (shakedown).
Pudgy twelve-year-olds in Union Jack shorts addicted to
coffee-whitener and frankfurters. And those boys who said,
'Hey, mister, we just want your car 'cos we're taking a girl
to the reservoir,' are outside the pub. Fine figures of men;
exercising and dieting just doesn't suit them. 'Have a meal in
a glass, we're having a laugh, just come over here and your
face we will smash.'

Oh God! You'd better leave town before you get caught in
the Catcliffe Shakedown.

Oh no, it's not that bad really: not if you've been living in
Bosnia for the last year. Home brew is still big news round
these parts – no airing cupboard should be without it. They
were going to open an airport – can you imagine it? 'Whilst
in the area why not stock up on string or try some of our
duty-free parkin?' Oh yeah. Let's go.

See the rainbow high above the viaduct, glowing with all the colours of a bottle of spilt milk. Oh, it's so beautiful, but I don't know what it means. Oh, rainbow high above – what exactly are you advertising?

And our idea of sophisticated humour is setting fire to our farts with disposable lighters. Why not try our delicious lager-style drink with a chocolate-flavoured candy-covered biscuit? *'Look at those buttercups over there, Mummy!'* *'Hold one under your chin.' 'What's butter, Mummy?' 'Oh, it's just a different make of margarine.'*

See the rainbow high above the viaduct, glowing with all the colours of a bottle of spilt milk. Oh, it's so beautiful, but I don't know what it means. Oh, rainbow high above – what exactly are you advertising?

The film now cuts to reveal who is watching this docudrama: A middle-class couple sit in wonder as the titles roll. 'All nicotine stains and beer bellies in this programme were real.'

But upstairs in his room, amongst the Airfix planes, is a small boy. He sits in the dark, listening for the sound of the train that crosses the viaduct at four o'clock every morning. The train that carries the dismembered remains – the dismembered remains of Matchstalk Men and Matchstalk Cats and Dogs, and it's coming,
and it's coming, coming . . .
*'What you looking at?' 'I don't know – label's fell off.' 'I'm going aht.' 'Am I so beautiful you can't stop looking at me?' 'Am I so beautiful?' 'You don't scare me.' 'I'll take you all on.' 'You and whose army?' 'Me – me and my fist-y.'*

Catcliffe, you don't intimidate me, your Parkway and your shopping centre, your Panda Pops and pottery, your

motorway junction, overwhelming stench of failure. Lives that never left first base, stunted by vapours from the cooling towers. And I will do everything in my power to get away from you.
Oh yeah.

# P.T.A. (Parent Teacher Association)

I know I'm getting on and you're so very young, but would
you like to stay till next Saturday?
Or Sunday?

I'll give you your own room – it's next door to my room –
and some time in the night, well, maybe I just might . . .

Take your clothes off, won't you, please?
You don't have to talk to me.
Just leave the light on so I can see you've got everything I
need.

You know, I can't forget that special night we met at the local
P.T.A. when your mother came to say that you'd been taking
days off school. I turned and looked at you and said,
'Yes, I understand.
I'm going to take this girl in hand.'

Take your clothes off – one, two, three.
No, you don't have to talk to me.
Just leave the light on so I can see you've got everything you
need.

Hit me

'Cos I never had a woman before:
I was too scared to touch the girls at the Poly
And I don't know what it's like to be young 'cos all my life
I've been knocking on forty.
Oh yeah.

JARVIS: So if I put my hand on your bosom . . .

CANDIDA: Yeah?

JARVIS: Will that give you an orgasm? No, that's not right.
But if we kiss with tongues . . .

CANDIDA: (*laughs*)

JARVIS: Won't that make you pregnant?

Just one touch was all it took.
You can't learn it from a book.
Let's go upstairs and have a . . . look.
Yes, you've got everything I need.

Hit me.

# Set the Controls for the Heart of the Pelvis

(Save me from my own hand.)
(Now my guard's down.)

Set the controls for the heart of the pelvis. Haven't you heard
my name rhymes with Elvis? And one thing I know is this:
that your mouth is telling me to give you a big kiss.

(Save me from my own hand.)
(Now my guard's down.)

Can't you see what's on offer? Yeah, babe, it's going cheap
today. I enter a room and all the girls say, 'C'mon, Jarv, can
I be the first? Oh, you make us so hot we feel we're gonna
burst.' Oh yeah . . .

So please don't leave me alone in this double bed. It smells
of damp towels and asthma inhalers. Say you're going to call
back later. Save me from these glossy photographs. Save me
from my mother's laugh. Save me. That's right, girls. Save me
from my own hand . . . C'mon . . . c'mon . . . c'mon . . . Do
you know how much I want you? Don't stop.

## Cocaine Socialism

I thought that you were joking when you said,
'I want to see you to discuss your contribution to the future
of our nation's heart and soul.
Six o'clock, my place, Whitehall.'

Well, I arrived just after seven,
but you said, 'It doesn't matter, I understand your situation
and your image and I'm flattered.
Oh, I'd just like to tell you that I love all of your albums.
Could you sign this for my daughter?
She's in hospital, her name is Miriam.
Now I'll get down to the gist: do you want a line of this?
Are you a [*sniff*] socialist?'

Now I'm doing fine –
buzzzzin' all the time.
Just one hit and I feel great –
and I support the Welfare State.
'Ah, you must be a socialist 'cos you're always off out on the
piss in your private members' bar.
Oh yes, you are, you superstar!'

'Well you sing about "common people" and the "mis-shapes
and the misfits", so can you bring them to my party and get
them all to sniff this?
And all I'm really saying is, "Come on and rock the vote for
me."
All I'm really saying is, "Come on, roll up that note for me."
Your choice in all of this is:
do you want hits, or do you want misses?
Are you a socialist – yeah?'

'Oh, you can be just what you want to be, just as long as you don't try to compete with me.

And we've waited such a long time for the chance to help our own kind, so now please come on and toe the party line.

Oh, you owe it to yourself.

Don't think of anybody else

and we promise we won't tell.

We won't tell.

No, we won't tell.'

## Glory Days

Come and play the tunes of glory. Raise your voice in
celebration of the days that we have wasted in the cafe, in
the station, and learn the meaning of existence in fortnightly
instalments. Come share this golden age with me in my
single-room apartment, and if it all amounts to nothing it
doesn't matter – these are still our glory days.

Oh, my face is unappealing and my thoughts are unoriginal.
I did experiments with substances but all it did was make me
ill. And I used to do the *I Ching* but then I had to feed the
meter, now I can't see into the future but at least I can use
the heater. Oh, it doesn't get much better than this 'cos this is
how we live our glory days.

Oh, and I could be a genius if I just put my mind to it. And I,
I could do anything if only I could get a Round Tuit. Oh, we
were brought up on the Space Race, now they expect you to
clean toilets. When you have seen how big the world is, how
can you make do with this? If you want me, I'll be sleeping
in, sleeping in throughout these glory days.

These glory days can take their toll, so catch me now before I
turn to gold. Yeah, we'd love to hear your story, just as long
as it tells us that where we are is where we're meant to be.
Oh, come on – make it up yourself: you don't need anybody
else. And I promise I won't sell these days to anybody else in
the world but you.
No one but you.

# Help the Aged

Help the aged,
one time they were just like you:
drinking,
smoking cigs
and sniffing glue.

Help the aged,
don't just put them in a home:
can't have much fun in there all on their own.
Give a hand, if you can –
try and help them to unwind.
Give them hope and give them comfort
'cos they're running out of time.

In the meantime we try –
try to forget that nothing lasts for ever.
No big deal, so give us all a feel.
Funny how it all falls away.
When did you first realise it's time you took an older lover,
baby?
Teach you stuff, although he's looking rough.
Funny how it all falls away

Help the aged
'cos one day you'll be older too.
You might need someone who can pull you through,
and if you look very hard behind those lines upon their face
you may see where you are headed,
and it's such a lonely place.
Oh.

In the meantime we try –
try to forget that nothing lasts for ever.
No big deal, so give us all a feel.
Funny how it all falls away.
When did you first realise it's time you took an older lover,
baby?
Teach you stuff, although he's looking rough.
Funny how it all falls away.

You can dye your hair but it's the one thing you can't change:
can't run away from yourself.

In the meantime we try . . .

So help the aged.

## This Is Hardcore

You are Hardcore.
You make me hard.
You name the drama, and I'll play the part.

It seems I saw you in some teenage wet dream.
I like your get-up, if you know what I mean.

I want it bad,
I want it now.
Oh, can't you see I'm ready now?

I've seen all the pictures,
I've studied them for ever.
I wanna make a movie, so let's star in it together.
Don't make a move till I say 'Action'.

Here comes the Hardcore Life.

Put your money where your mouth is tonight.
Leave your make-up on and I'll leave on the light.
Come over here, babe, and talk in the mic.
Oh yeah – I hear you now –
It's gonna be one hell of a night.

You can't be a spectator – oh no.
You've got to take these dreams and make them whole.

This is Hardcore:
there is no way back for you.
This is Hardcore:
this is me on top of you.
And I can't believe that it took me this long.

That it took me this long.

This is the eye of the storm,
it's what men in stained raincoats pay for
but in here it is pure.

This is the end of the line.
I've seen the storyline played out so many times before:

That goes in there,
then that goes in there,
then that goes in there,
then that goes in there,
and then it's over.

Oh, what a hell of a show,
but what I want to know:
What exactly do you do for an encore?

'Cos this is Hardcore.

# The Professional

I'm back in full effect,
can't even hold myself erect.
I've got nothing that I want to say,
I'm gonna say it anyway.
I know you think that I've lost it, baby,
I know you think that my star is fading.
Used to be a contender, now you're just a pretender.
Psychic karaoke every weekend.
You don't fit those clothes any more.
Why don't you take them back to the charity store?
While you're there you could always hand yourself in.
You're into green issues – start recycling.
You hide behind your woman when you're out on the town,
show her up and slag her off for holding you down,
holding you down,
holding you down.
You're the only one who's holding you down.
You're only ever polite when you're out of your box.
And Cocker's short for ****sucker:
a sucker of . . .
a sucker of . . .

When I got up today I had that feeling again.
Everything was okay then the world started seeping in.
Now I'm trying to sleep it away but I can't sleep it away.
Can you answer this question?
Can you answer it right?
Have you ever done anything good in your life?
Have you ever done anything that wasn't just for yourself?
Are you capable of giving?
Capable of giving just for the sake of it, without expecting
anything in return?

I'm only trying to give you what you've come to expect:
just another song about single mothers and sex,
single mothers and sex,
single mothers and sex.
This is a song about single mothers and sex.
Okay, you've heard it before – it's nothing special,
but it's a living, can't you see?
And I'm a Professional.
Yeah, I'm a Professional.

Sleep on, my darling.
Sleep on, don't wake as I leave.
I've been rehearsing this scene so long now,
don't interrupt me as I do it for real.
The bedroom floor is treacherous
A tea cup could be disastrous 'cos that would mean I would
have to say what was written on the letter I posted yesterday
so that it would get here when I was gone and you awoke.

Oh, she will meet me from the train and she won't know a
thing about how I talk with my mouth full and only bath
once a week. How I'm nicer the first time you meet me than
the next. And how I'm rapidly losing interest in sex. Yeah,
I'm rapidly losing interest in sex.

What's the point in making it overemotional?
You can do it the hard way –
or you can be a Professional.
I'm a Professional.

Sleep on, my darling.
Sleep on, my love.

## Laughing Boy

If you stay out all night,
that's alright by me,
but if you must kiss those guys
you could at least clean your teeth.
I don't mean to put you down,
but you've taken everything that I own.
Don't tell me you want some more 'cos I'm closed.
Yeah, I'm closed.
Yeah, I'm closed.

Who is this laughing boy who ladders your tights?
Please tell him to cut the noise
'cos it's spoiling my nights.
I just want to get some rest
and he's talking to his ma on the phone.
Well, if he's so homesick he could go home.
He could go home.
He could go home.

I don't need this any more, and it's written in the stars I must
go.

And will I come back for more? I don't know.

# The Fear

This is our 'Music From a Bachelor's Den', the sound of
loneliness turned up to ten. A horror soundtrack from a
stagnant waterbed, and it sounds just like this. This is the
sound of someone losing the plot, making out that they're
okay when they're not. You're gonna like it – but not a lot,
and the chorus goes like this:

Here comes the fear again.
The end is near again.
A monkey's built a house on your back.
You can't get anyone to come in the sack,
and here comes another panic attack.
Here we go again.

So now you know the words to our song pretty soon you'll
all be singing along. When you're sad, when you're lonely
and it all turns out wrong. When you've got the fear. And
when you're no longer searching for beauty or love – just
some kind of life with the edges taken off. When you can't
even define what it is that you are frightened of – this song
will be here:

Here comes the fear again.
The end is near again.
If you ever get that chimp off your back,
if you ever find the thing that you lack,
but you know you're only having a laugh,
and here we go again
until the end.

Until the end.

# Dishes

I am not Jesus, though I have the same initials.
I am the man who stays home and does the dishes.
And how was your day?
Is that woman still trying to do your head in?

A man told me to beware of thirty-three.
He said, 'It was not an easy time for me.'
But I'll get through, even though I've got no miracles to show
you.

I'd like to make this water wine but it's impossible –
I've got to get these dishes dry.

I'll read a story if it helps you sleep at night.
I've got some matches if you ever need a light.
Oh, I am just a man but I am doing what I can to help you.

I'd like to make this water wine but it's impossible –
I've got to get these dishes dry.

And I'm not worried that I will never touch the stars
'cos stars belong up in heaven
and the Earth is where we are.

And aren't you happy just to be alive?
Anything's possible.
You've got no cross to bear tonight.
No, not tonight.

I am not Jesus, though I have the same initials.

## Party Hard

I used to try very hard to make friends with everyone on the
planet.
I've seen you havin' it,
havin' it,
but now you've just had it.
Entertainment can sometimes be hard when the thing that
you love is the same thing that's holding you down.

This man is dangerous,
he just shed his load on your best party frock.
Before you enter the palace of wisdom you have to decide:
are you ready to rock?
Can you party with me?
Can you show me a good time?
Do you even know what one looks like?
And I don't need to hear your stories again,
just get on the floor and show me –
show me what you're made of.
Just what exactly are you made of?

Baby, you're driving me crazy.
Baby, you're driving me crazy.

I was having a whale of a time until your uncle Psychosis
arrived.
Why do we have to half kill ourselves just to prove we're
alive?
I'm here whenever you need me, and whenever you need me I
won't be here.
And did you ever stop to ask yourself?
'If you didn't come to party, then why did you come here?'

Why did you come here?

Baby, you're driving me crazy.
Baby, you're driving me crazy.

And do you really want to know just how come you turned
out so dumb?

When the party's over will you come home with me?
Now the party's over will you come home to me?
Will you come home to me?

# TV Movie

Without you my life has become a hangover without end.
A movie made for TV: bad dialogue, bad acting, no interest –
too long with no story . . . and no sex.

Is it a kind of weakness to miss someone so much?
To wish the day would go away?
Like you did yesterday.
Just like you did yesterday.

And I can't think of a way to get through this pain:
To be happy again, to make it all alright
and I know it must be bad because sitting here right now all I
know is I can't even think of anything clever to say.

So I say: 'Why pretend any longer?
'Cos I need you here with me.
It's obvious that I miss you so much,
so please say you're going to stay.
Please say you're going to stay.'

The night is getting darker now and there's nothing on TV,
but I'll sit tight till morning light: I'll wait until the day –
until the day that you say you're going to stay.

# A Little Soul

Hey, man, how come you treat your woman so bad? That's
not the way you do it. No, no, no, no, you shouldn't do
it like that. I could show you how to do it right. I used to
practise every night on my wife – now she's gone. Yeah, she's
gone. You see your mother and me we never got along that
well, you see. I'd love to help you 'cos everybody's telling me:

You look like me, but please don't turn out like me.
You look like me, but you're not like me, I know.
I had one, two, three, four shots of happiness.
I look like a big man but I've only got a little soul,
I only got a little soul.

Yeah, I wish I could be an example. I wish I could say I stood
up for you and fought for what was right but I never did. I
just wore my trench coat and stayed out every single night.
You think I'm joking? Hey – try me.

Yeah, come on, try me tonight.
I did what was wrong though I knew what was right.
I've got no wisdom that I want to pass on.
Just don't hang round here, no, I'm telling you, son:
you don't wanna know me.
Oh, that's just what everybody's telling me.

And everybody's telling me you look like me, but please
don't turn into me. You look like me, but you're not like me,
I hope, 'cos I have run away from the one thing that I ever
made. Now I only wish that I could show you,
wish I could show a little soul.

# Modern Marriage

I promise not to rip you off. And I promise not to sell you out. I will never smoke all your stash if I happen to find it whilst tidying up. Which, let's face it, isn't likely. Well, I would always leave you at least a joint's worth, anyway. And I will never eat the last bit of cereal and then put the empty packet back, hoping you won't notice, or if I do, I'll pay for the next lot, I promise, 'cos I know that really gets on your nerves. And I will never sleep with any of your friends – well, not your best friends.

I don't know just what I'm meant to do, I don't want to make it wrong for you. How can we escape what's happened to all those others who've gone before us two? Baby, we have lived together, now we'll do it all for ever. Hold my hand, don't ever let it go. Close your eyes, hold tight, and here we go.

And how do we avoid being like all those other cheese-masters? Demonstrating the facilities of their new car and the trouser press. From hunter-gatherer to washer-dryer is a long, strange trip. And what if our kids turn into pudgy blobs, wearing Union Jack underpants, addicted to coffee-whitener? Bloated caricatures of something vaguely recognisable as a human being. A human being that you once loved.

I don't know just what I'm meant to do. I don't want to make it wrong for you. How can we escape what's happened to all those others who've gone before us two? Baby, we have lived together, now we'll do it all for ever. Hold my hand, don't ever let it go. Close your eyes, hold tight, and here we go.

So this is it: we're walking down the aisle, the dawning of a new era. Is this the start of a new airbrushed Disney-life or some thirty-six-part depressing-as-hell northern drama to be repeated every night for the rest of our lives? Oh, and now I'm frightened. Oh yeah, I'm shitting Barratt houses here. Is this the right thing? And then suddenly I'm turning to look at your face and I'm saying, 'I do,' 'I do,' 'I do.'

I do.

# First Man in Space

*Dear Mary,*

> *So nice to be back on solid ground after being away for so long. Gravity's a drag though isn't it? Really gets me down sometimes. I hardly recognised the place when I first got back – I still feel slightly dislocated. Whilst I was exploring the final frontier there seems to have been a Coffee Revolution: now everyone's a Rocket man – as long as it's served with a balsamic dressing. But I musn't complain: so many others didn't make it back or never even got off the ground in the first place. Please call round whenever you feel like it, it'd be lovely to see you again. The kids must be quite grown up now I suppose. Still – that's progress for you.*
> *See you soon.*
> *Love, Phil xx*

I was the first man in space on my street.
I had to leave my wife and kids behind.
It was a chance I could not pass up on:
it was the journey of a lifetime.

I threw away my packing-up as they were waving me bye bye.
Sometimes all I need is the air that I breathe
And the air that I breathe is so thin I get high.

And I'm floating like God in his heaven,
High in the stratosphere.
Darling, come quick, you can see our house from here.

Seen some burn-up on re-entry,
bones that have crumbled to dust.
It was rough but I kept it together,

but now I'm finding it hard to adjust:
how're you supposed to open these new milk cartons?
Why don't they make Golden Nuggets no more?
Where was the ticker-tape civic reception?
How come no one wants to know what I saw?
How come no one wants to know what I saw?
How come no one wants to know?

And I'm floating like God in his heaven,
High in the stratosphere.
Darling, come quick, you can see our house from here.

Lumps of rock
Alien life forms
Parties with no atmosphere
Space is cold
Home is colder
When you come home at night and there's nobody here,
when you come home at night and there's nobody here . . .

And I'm floating like God in his heaven.

## Stars on Sunday

How can a child grow up to be straight and tall
in this sad imitation of life?
It's no good at all.
No Christmas illuminations dance in their eyes.
They were sold off to Patnicks.
Oh, what a surprise.

Gaze into the sky.
Maybe we can get there one day.
Meanwhile we spend our time watching
*Stars on Sunday*.

Sing 'hallelujah' for the old folks
balling the jack in a granny flat.
Singing the songs that they used to sing
but where is the sense in that?
The chicken has flown the basket and is now cooped up
indoors.
Someone is crying deep in the night, 'Just what are we living
for?'

Gaze into the sky.
Maybe we can get there one day.
Meanwhile we spend our time watching
*Stars on Sunday*.

Watching *Stars on Sunday*.

# The Quiet Revolution

You never saw my *Hamlet*,
and it was something to see.
Hiding under a duvet cover,
tragically.
My *Macbeth* was an error of judgement.
No one wants to see my *Lear* –
the Quiet Revolution's here.

In domestic dramas all across the nation
gifted amateurs tread the boards all night,
full of inner motivation.
'Is this a microwave I see before me?'
As the clock strikes 3 a.m.
Thus it would appear.
I can hardly wait for my fate to appear.
The Quiet Revolution's here.

Oh, but you keep on rocking,
even though your friends are dropping dead like flies
or wearing stockings.
Keep rocking,
yeah, yeah, yeah.

You could have heard a pin drop at Gatecrasher last
Thursday at 4 a.m.: People dancing to the rhythm of their
own heartbeats, 140 bpm. Oh, you've got to slow down, my
son, if you wanna know just what's happening here.
The Quiet Revolution is here.

Yeah, I've seen how the world ends, And it's not with a
bang but a whisper, and nobody providing an emotional

commentary. What are you gonna do with the rest of your
life now there's never nothing good on TV? If all the world's
a stage, you may as well be the star of your own play
'cos the Quiet Revolution is here to stay.

Or you could keep on rocking,
Even though your friends are dropping dead like flies
or wearing stockings.
Yeah, keep rocking,
yeah, yeah, yeah.

Shhh . . .
the Quiet Revolution is here.

# The Trees

I took an air rifle,
shot a magpie to the ground,
and it died without a sound.

Your skin so pale against the fallen autumn leaves,
and no one saw us but the trees.

Yeah, the trees,
those useless trees produce the air that I am breathing.
Yeah, the trees,
those useless trees, they never said that you were leaving.

I carved your name with a heart just up above.
Now swollen, distorted, unrecognisable – like our love.

The smell of leaf mould and the sweetness of decay
are the incense at the funeral procession here today.

In the trees,
those useless trees produce the air that I am breathing.
Yeah, the trees,
those useless trees, they never said that you were leaving.

You try to shape the world to what you want the world to
be.
Carving your name a thousand times won't bring you back
to me.
Oh no.
I might as well just go and tell it to the trees.

Go and tell it to the trees.

## Weeds II (The Origin of the Species)

This is the true story of the weeds,
the origin of the species.
A story of cultivation, exploitation, civilisation.

Found flowering on wasteland unnoticed, unofficial,
accidental, a cutting was taken, but weeds do not thrive in
hothouse conditions and wilt when in competition with more
exotic strains.

A charming naivety, very short flowering season,
no sooner has the first blooming begun than decay sets in.

Bring your camera, take a photo of life on the margins,
offer money in exchange for sex and then get a taxi home.

The story has always been the same: a source of wonder due
to their ability to thrive on poor-quality soil offering very
little nourishment.
Drinking Nurishment.

But weeds must be kept under strict control or they will
destroy everything in their path.

Growing wild, then harvested in their prime and passed
around at dinner parties. 'Care for some weed?' So natural,
so wild, so unrefined, and someone's gonna make a fortune
one day, if only they can market this stuff right.

Come on,
do your dance.

Come on,
do your funny little dance.

Germination. Plantation. Exploitation. Civilisation.

A sensational buzz – zzzzzz.

Crop rotation. Genetic modification. The creation of
expectation. Ultimate frustration.

This is the story of the weeds,
the origin of the species.

# Wickerman

Just behind the station before you reach the traffic island a
river runs through a concrete channel. I took you there once;
I think it was after the Leadmill. The water was dirty and it
smelt of industrialisation. Little mesters coughing their lungs
up and globules the colour of tomato ketchup. But it flows.
Yeah, it flows.

Underneath the city through dirty brickwork conduits
connecting white witches on the Moor with Pre-Raphaelites
down in Broomhall. Beneath the old Trebor factory that
burnt down in the early seventies leaving an antiquated
sweet-shop smell and caverns of nougat and caramel.
Nougat. Yeah, nougat and caramel.

And the river flows on.

Yeah, the river flows on beneath pudgy fifteen-year-olds
addicted to coffee-whitener, courting couples naked on
Northern Upholstery and pensioners gathering dust like
bowls of plastic tulips. And it finally comes above ground
again at Forge Dam, the place where we first met.

I went there again for old times' sake, hoping to find
the child's toy-horse ride that played such a ridiculously
tragic tune. It was still there – but none of the kids seemed
interested in riding on it. And the cafe was still there too;
the same press-in plastic letters on the price list and scuffed
formica-top tables. I sat as close as possible to the seat
where I'd met you that autumn afternoon. And then, after
what seemed like hours of thinking about it, I finally took
your face in my hands and I kissed you for the first time

and a feeling like electricity flowed through my whole body. And I immediately knew I'd entered a completely different world. And all the time, in the background, the sound of that ridiculously heartbreaking child's ride outside.

At the other end of town the river flows underneath an old railway viaduct; I went there with you once – except you were somebody else – and we gazed down at the sludgy brown surface of the water together. Then a passer-by told us that it used to be a local custom to jump off the viaduct into the river, when coming home from the pub on a Saturday night, but that this custom had died out when someone jumped and landed too near to the riverbank and had sunk in the mud there and drowned before anyone could reach them. Maybe he'd just made the whole story up – but you'd never get me to jump off that bridge. No chance. Never in a million years.

Yeah, a river flows underneath this city.
I'd like to go there with you now, my pretty,
and follow it on for miles and miles below other people's
ordinary lives, occasionally catching a glimpse of the moon
through manhole covers along the route.
Yeah, it's dark sometimes, but if you hold my hand I think I
know the way.

This is as far as we got last time,
but if we go just another mile
we will surface surrounded by grass and trees
and the flyover that takes the cars to cities.
Buds that explode at the slightest touch.
Nettles that sting – but not too much.
I've never been past this point.
What lies ahead I really could not say.

And I used to live just by the river in a disused factory just
off the Wicker.
And the river flowed by day after day.
And 'One day,' I thought,
'one day I will follow it.'
But that day never came;
I moved away and lost track
but tonight I am thinking about making my way back.
I may find you there
and float on wherever the river may take me,
wherever the river may take me,
wherever the river may take us,
wherever it wants us to go.
Wherever it wants us to go.

# Bad Cover Version

Oh, the word's on the street: you've found someone new.
If he looks nothing like me, I'm so happy for you.
I heard an old girlfriend has turned to the Church.
She's trying to replace me but it'll never work.

'Cos every touch reminds you of just how sweet it could have
been and every time he kisses you it leaves behind the bitter
taste of saccharine.

A bad cover version of love is not the real thing.
Bikini-clad girl on the front who invited you in.
Such great disappointment when you got him home.
The original was so good, the one you no longer own.

And every touch reminds you of just how sweet it could
have been and every time he kisses you, you get the taste of
saccharine.
It's not easy to forget me –
it's so hard to disconnect. When it's electronically reprocessed
to give a more life-like effect.

Ah, sing your song about all the sad imitations that got it so
wrong.

It's like:
a later *Tom and Jerry* when the two of them could talk;
like the Stones since the eighties;
like the last days of Southfork;
like *Planet of the Apes* on TV;
the second side of *'Til the Band Comes In*;
like an own-brand box of cornflakes –
he's going to let you down, my friend.

# The Last Day of the Miners' Strike

Kids are spitting on the town-hall steps and frightening old
ladies. I dreamt that I was living back in the mid-1980s.
People marching, people shouting, people wearing pastel
leather. The future's ours for the taking now, if we just stick
together.

And I said, 'Hey, lay your burden down;
seems the last day of the miners' strike was the Magna Carta
in this part of town.'

Well, my body sank below the ground, it became as black
as night. Overhead, the sound of horses' hooves – people
fighting for their lives. Some joker in a headband was still
getting chicks for free and Big Brother was still watching you,
back in the days of '83.

And I said, 'Hey, lay your burden down –
seems the last day of the miners' strike was the Magna Carta
in this part of town.'

Well, by 1985, I was as cold as cold could be, but no one
was working underground to dig me out and set me free. '87
socialism gave way to socialising – so put your hands up in
the air once more: the North is rising.

And I said, 'Hey, lay your burden down,
seems the last day of the miners' strike was the Magna Carta
in this part of town.'

Oh, sing hallelujah.

By now I'm sick and tired of just living in this hole so I took
the ancient tablets, blew off the dust, swallowed them whole.
Come on, let's get together. Come on, the past is gone. Well,
the very first commandment: Come on, let's get it on.

Hey, lay your burden down,
seems the last day of the miners' strike was the Magna Carta
in this part of town.

# B-Real

Be real.
Grow hairs and be real 'cos I'm the real deal.
Feel me, feel me – I'm for real,
I'm for real.

Gonna get in shape.
Gonna cut down the drink.
Gonna exercise.
Spend time with the kids.
It's not too late to make things right.
Stay at home every other night.
Improve my mind.
Read a book.
Spend quality time.
Learn to cook.
Learn about wine.
Deal with bills
and deal with damp.

Be real.
Grow hairs and be real 'cos I'm the real deal.
Feel me, feel me – I'm for real,
I'm for real.

Get really excited about doing something worthwhile.
Really committed –
going the extra mile.
A really healthy lifestyle.
No, for real.
You're real; drink real ale.
Keep music live.

Come over here, I'll show you real life.
You're just playing at it, trying it out.
You dress like your dad, how's the wife?
You want something real?
You want some real pain? Well, try this for size.
You want some real pain? Try this for size.

Be real.
Grow hairs and be real 'cos I'm the real deal.
Feel me, feel me I'm for real,
I'm for real.

You want something real?
You want something raw?
Try this for size:
pick your teeth off the floor.
I saw it on *Later*,
so I got the CD.
Stone-baked pizza.
Oh deary me,
oh deary me,
are you for real?

DJs, late bar, stone-baked pizza.
DJs, late bar, stone-baked pizza.
Modern-day dinner-dance.
Keep it real for the fans.

Body-warmers in the pub? Be real.
Trendy gets with home-cut hair? Be real.
This game's got brilliant graphics? Be real. Be real.

Be real.
Grow hairs and be real 'cos I'm the real deal.
Feel me, feel me I'm for real,
I'm for real.

# Mary

Mary, I just called to tell you that both our children are on
drugs and the way that things are going they'll be dead long
before either one of us. Last night I saw Darren, he didn't
recognise me – he offered me out. Didn't recognise his own
father. Tell me, Mary – what's that all about?

Mary, I'm sorry, Mary, I'm scared,
Mary, I still love you, Mary – are you there?

Mary.

Now I – I like a bit of fun now and then and I know
sometimes I have too much. And I know things are different
now – but drugs, Mary! Fucking drugs!

Mary, I'm sorry, Mary, I'm scared,
Mary, I still love you, Mary – are you there?

Okay – I haven't kept up with the payments.
Okay – I know I wasn't always there.
Okay – yeah, I could lose a little weight
but, Mary – tell me that you care.

Mary, I'm sorry, Mary, I'm scared,
Mary, I still love you.

Mary – are you there?

# Sliding Through Life on Charm

The family tree was chainsawed Wednesday week,
so now I have to mingle with the meek.
Hey, mister, you have finally met your match.
Now everybody wants to kiss my snatch,
to go where God knows who has gone before.
I am a muse, not a mistress, not a whore.
Suburban shits who want some class all queue up to kiss my
ass. And I was only trying to please: I never got any royalties.
Oh no, not me: I'm still sliding through life on charm.
Sliding through life on charm.

If Marianne was born a man she'd show you all the way to
piss your life against the wall.
Go ahead, why don't you leave me to these thugs?
And creeps who want to fuck a nun – on drugs.
Is it a sin I never ever tried too hard?
I had to know how far was going too far.
In proper homes throughout the land fathers try to
understand why Eunice, who is seventeen, aspires to live her
life like me.
Oh – can't you see, Daddy? She's just captivated by my
charm.
Sliding through life on charm.

I wonder why the schools don't teach anything useful
nowadays? Like how to fall from grace and slide with
elegance from a pedestal I never asked to be on in the first
place . . . Sliding on charm.

# The Operation

I want to explore you, I'm going to get under your skin so
you can feel me running through your veins.

I want to examine every inch of your frame, the pressure
points that cause you joy and pain.

Our love goes under the knife.
There is no room for doubt.

Now I'm inside you my hands can feel their way, further
inside than I have ever been. Now I can really mess around
with your heart and fill it to the brim with broken dreams.

Our love goes under the knife.
Two lives may be saved.

And if I pull this off I will refuse the Nobel Prize.
Instead I will look into your eyes.
And if I pull this off, your whole body will be mine,
and I'm prepared to work throughout the night.

Our love goes under the knife.
Nothing is taboo,
here on the cutting edge of science.

Too much information, I feel I'm getting lost, absorbed into
the fibre of your soul.

Deep within the abattoir of your entrails, your insides, lost in
you for ever, far from home.

Our love goes under the knife.
Someone got too close.

Our love goes under the knife.
The heart was rejected by the host.

# Set Yourself on Fire

Now come and stand,
see the sights and warm your hands
and fan the flame inside of me.

Been burning all my life,
so come and set my house alight,
come and set my spirit free.

Now all is ashes,
this moribund parade of asses,
so shake it one more time for me.

So take these matches off of me and set yourself on fire.

Coffee at the Flore,
it seemed just like the day before.
The waiter winked and smiled at me.
'The couple at the bar?
He burned his bridges,
she burned her bra,
now somebody has burned their car.'

Sulphur in the air and cracks appearing everywhere,
don't try to stop it, don't you dare.

Now see that everything must fall that we may live again.

So take these matches off of me and set yourself on fire.

Now it's so clear to me,
this bonfire of the vanities,

so come on everybody – scream.

A purifying flame,
and you and I can take the blame,
a spirit that cannot be tamed.

Now see that everything must fall that we may live again.

So take these matches off of me and set yourself on fire.

# Cunts Are Still Running the World

Well, did you hear there's a natural order?
Those most deserving will end up with the most?
That the cream cannot help but always rise up to the top?
Well, I say, 'Shit floats.'

If you thought things had changed –
friend, you'd better think again.
Bluntly put, in the fewest of words.
Cunts are still running the world,
Cunts are still running the world.

Now the working classes are obsolete,
they are surplus to society's needs.
So let them all kill each other and get it made overseas.
That's the word, don't you know?
From the guys that's running the show.
Let's be perfectly clear, boys and girls.
Cunts are still running the world,
Cunts are still running the world.

Well, feed your children on crayfish and lobster tails.
Find a school near the top of the league.
In theory, I respect your right to exist;
I will kill you if you move in next to me.
And it stinks,
and it sucks,
it's anthropologically unjust
but the takings are up by a third.
So Cunts are still running the world.
Yeah, Cunts are still running the world.

The free market is perfectly natural.
Do you think that I'm some kind of dummy?
It's the ideal way to order the world:
Fuck the morals – does it make any money?

And if you don't like it then leave,
or use your right to protest on the street.
Yeah, use your right but don't imagine that it's heard –
not whilst cunts are still running the world.

Cunts are still running the world.

## Disney Time

How come they're called 'adult movies' when the only thing they show is people making babies filmed up close? I'm feeling so much better since I learned to avert my eyes; now it's Disney time.

Not in front of the children. Fill their head with dreams and hope to be like Bambi's mother and die off-screen. So you can tell your children that everything's gonna be just fine – here in Disney time.

At Easter and Christmas they granted us a view of a world so much better than the one we knew. Everyone can share the magic – for thirty minutes at a time – here in Disney time.

Here in Disney time.

# Big Julie

'*It happened that green and crazy summer. It was a summer
when for a long time she had not been a member. She
belonged to no club and she was a member of nothing in the
world. And she was afraid.*'

She's by herself again in the quiet secret night
below the neighbour's window.
Hands in pockets, head on one side,
and the radio plays an unknown song that has nothing at all
to do with God.
But it's miles away from this sad town and the stupid kids
who get her down.
Just wait until Big Julie rules the world,
Big Julie rules the world.

Well, the radio still plays,
floating beyond time like the greatest people in the world all
springing up and feeling fine.
And it's far away from these sweaty lads who say that boys
cannot be slags.
And if it's not them then it's their dads –
like the guy who felt her up in class
and Sunday-school teacher who said she had beautiful breasts
and the local-radio DJ who is so obviously obsessed.
Yeah, form an orderly queue when Big Julie rules the world,
Big Julie rules the world.

Yeah, go and chase your dreams.
But if your dreams are not your own then wouldn't it be
better just to work things out at home?

And she knows that sex is just for dummies anyway,
something you do when you've run out of things to say.
But this song will play until the light,
it's the sound of her trying to find something to like –
the sound of her walking day and night.
And this song may lead her far away but tonight it seems to
light the way and she can almost see the future shine.
And everything's in tune and everything's in time.
And it will play until the day Big Julie rules the world.

Big Julie rules the world.

# I Will Kill Again

Build yourself a castle.
Keep your family safe from harm.
Get into classical music.
Raise rabbits on a farm.
Log on in the night-time.
Drink a half-bottle of wine.
Buy a couple of records.
Look at naked girls from time to time.

And people tell me what a real nice guy you are, so come on,
serenade me on your acoustic guitar. And don't believe me if
I claim to be your friend, 'cos given half the chance I know
that I will kill again. I will kill again.

And wouldn't it be nice for all the world to live in peace?
And no one gets ill or ever dies –
or dies of boredom at the very least?

And people tell me what a real nice guy you are, so come on,
serenade me on your acoustic guitar. And don't believe me if
I claim to be your friend, 'cos given half the chance I know
that I will kill again. I will kill again.

## Fat Children

Last night I had a little altercation. They wobbled menacingly beneath the yellow street light. It became a situation.

Well, they wanted my brand-new phone with all the pictures of the kids and the wife. A struggle ensued and then fat children took my life.

Fat children took my life. Oh.

Well, some passers-by took me to the station. The police force was elsewhere, putting bullets in some guy's head for no particular reason. So I died in the back of the cab but I'll be back to haunt them. This thing does not end here: my spirit walks the streets of Tottenham.

Singing, 'Fat children took my life.' Oh.

Yeah, the parents are the problem: giving birth to maggots without the sense to become flies. So pander to your pampered little princess – of such enormous size.

## The Loss Adjuster

Sitting in the World's End with some indie friends, a
newsflash on the TV says the world's about to end. Can't
catch all the details 'cos the volume's turned down: this is the
last night on Earth – as spent in Camden Town.

There's no way to escape – this is it.
Tomorrow we will all be gone, so check what time the band
are on.
Let's go outside.

Yeah, and this was the night I was going to balance the
books; the night I turned a minus into a plus. The night my
adjustment became complete – I could start again with a
clean sheet. Now I can't get through 'cos all the networks
are down, and fires are starting all over town, and you're
probably being gang-banged by tattooed locals.
Damn those yokels!
Damn those yokels!

And a girl cries as she stumbles by, 'No, the world can't end
now – no, it's got to wait. It can't end when I haven't got a
boyfriend and I'm half a stone overweight.' The guys from
Arlington House are marauding the streets and convent girls
are screwing every man that they meet, and the album you
just bought will never get heard. Oh yeah, complete social
breakdown has occurred.

And then you find yourself thinking about Egyptian Sue and
the evil things that she used to do. And the night you almost
did it after the wedding reception but you didn't have any
contraception – and anyway, you couldn't get an erection.

Now, what the hell made you think of her? Could it be
that old saying coming true? That 'Nothing could survive a
nuclear holocaust except cockroaches and Egyptian Sue?' But
even Sue won't make it through. No, even Sue won't make it
through this time.

It was around this time that the levels of hysteria around
the Kentish Town Road caused a warping of the space–time
continuum and I found myself face to face with a version of
myself from fifteen years earlier, when I'd lived in the area.
'Greetings indie legend,' said I. 'Fuck off, sad bell-end,'
came the reply. I wanted to warn him about the rough times
ahead, but for some reason he had his coat pulled over his
head and wouldn't listen. I left him trying to extricate a
punctured Spacehopper from under some rubble in a skip.
'He'll find out soon enough,' I thought.

And then suddenly I realised that I could no longer breathe.

Here we go, move along, one last time.
The Loss Adjuster lost his mind: too many claims, too little
time to file them.

And then suddenly it was a Tuesday afternoon and I could
see it all, crystal clear; like a giant chandelier turning slowly
in the sideways sunlight – hanging by a thread with only
seconds to last. And each time you rang it was like an
Indian call centre on the line: 'Yes, I'm doing fine – just like
the last time, and the last time; make this the last time.'

We'll all be gone by Monday morning –
this is it: your final warning.
You never did see *Dog Day Afternoon*.
Here today but gone tomorrow –
now you could hang your head in sorrow or you could do it.
But you'd better do it soon.

# Fuckingsong

I will never get to touch you so I wrote this song instead:
thinking about you lying on my bed
(it's gonna get inside your head).
And it's the best that I can do,
this is the closest I could get,
so let it penetrate your –
consciousness,
oh yes.

Turn it up,
turn me on,
I'm feeling good but don't get me wrong:
I know it's just a song.

And every time you play it I will perform the best I can.
Press 'repeat'
and there I am,
and there I am,
always glad to be your man.
And this way there won't be any mess –
As I assure you that there would be in the flesh.
This is my very, very best.

Turn it up,
turn me on,
I'm feeling good but don't get me wrong:
I know it's just a song.

Always eager,
always ready,
always in tune and always primed.

And I'm always there for you,
and I'm always on time –
unlike in real life.

Turn it up,
turn me on,
I'm feeling good but don't get me wrong.
No, don't get me wrong,
'cos I know:
it's just a Fucking Song.

# I Never Said I Was Deep

I love your body 'cos I've lost my mind.
If you want someone to talk to, you're wasting your time.
If you want someone to share your life, you need someone
who's alive.
And if every relationship is a two-way street, I have been
screwing in the back whilst you drive.

I never said I was deep, but I am profoundly shallow.
My lack of knowledge is vast and my horizons are narrow.
I never said I was big,
I never said that I was clever.
And if you're waiting to find what's going on in my mind,
you could be waiting for ever.
For ever and ever.

I can't dance you to the end of the night
'cos I'm afraid of the dark.
I have to confess: I'm out of my depth.
You're going over my head and straight through my heart.

Some girls like to play it dirty, some girls want to be your
mum. Me, I disrespected you whilst we were waiting for
the taxi to come. My morality is shabby, my behaviour
unacceptable. No, I'm not looking for a relationship, just a
willing receptacle.

I never said I was . . .
I never said I was . . .
I never said I was . . .

I never said I was deep.

# Leftovers

I met her in the Museum of Palaeontology and I make no
bones about it: I said, 'If you wish to study dinosaurs, I know
a specimen whose interest is undoubted.'

Trapped in a body that is failing me please allow me to be
succinct: I wanna love you whilst we both still have flesh
upon our bones – before we both become extinct.

That's what I told her:
'I wanna be your lover.'
And then I told her twice:
'I wanna be your lover.'

Well, he says he loves you like a sister. Well, I guess that's
relative. He says that he wants to make love to you. But
instead of 'to', shouldn't that be 'with'?

And I told you once:
'I wanna be your lover.'
And now I've told you twice, Homes:
'I wanna be your lover.'

So I come to you filled with guilt and self-loathing and I am
praying that you could make me good. And so I fall upon
your neck just like a vampire. Yeah – like a vampire who
faints at the sight of blood.

And I told you once:
'I wanna be your lover.' (I'm gonna say it again.)
And then I told you twice:
'I wanna be your lover.'

Well, this is my CV and I've got no one else to blame,
so I will state my case,
Yes, I will state it again:

Come and help yourself to leftovers. I've got a little surplus
love and affection. I'm getting cuddly, so won't you cuddle
me? I could be your teddy bear, oh yeah. I know I ain't no
eligible bachelor, this is no mouth-watering proposition.
Make no mistake – you're in big trouble, little lady, if we
start a-huggin' and a-kissin', and a-kissin':
are you listening?

'Cos I told you once
and then I told you twice,
and now I've told you three times.
And at the risk of repeating myself I'm gonna say it again:

'I wanna be your lover.'
'I wanna be your lover.'

# Hold Still

The train was leaving in ten minutes or so.
Struggling with the suitcases I did not see you go.
My heart stopped beating and I felt my blood run cold.

'Hold still,' I told you, but you moved.
Now you're gone, I can't find you.

Growing.
Yeah, we are growing but why bother when you can hover?
Oh.
On your knees and behold the might of the master.
Eyes explode at the very sight of the master.
We're cosmic dust but you're everything to me.

Like a single parent at the fair and you're spinning above me.

Spinning.
Yes, you're moving fast but you're going nowhere.
Yeah, baby, that's the way.
Oh.
On your knees and behold the might of the master.
Eyes explode at the very sight of the master.
Kittens are cute but a full-grown cat can be cuter.
And I'm alive but I plan to die in the future.
Hold still,
hold still,
hold still.

We're cosmic dust but you're everything to me.

# You're in My Eyes (Discosong)

Grey floaters inside my eyes, visible when you look into a
clear blue sky. Memories of days gone by activated by a
mirror ball shining bright in a provincial disco on a Thursday
night.

You appeared from nowhere beside me on the floor, identical
in every detail to the way you were before. The best part of
a decade since you went out of my life. The worst part of a
decade – but here you are tonight by my side.

You're in my eyes,
you're in my face,
just like before you went away.
You're in my arms,
I feel your warmth,
and I will dance until the dawn
'cos I don't want to lose you again, oh no.

A trick of the light, a disco hallucination, a waking dream,
an impossible situation. Oh, but you look real good in your
halter-top – don't stop, don't disappear – I need you here.

I need you here.

You're in my eyes,
you're in my face,
just like before you went away.
You're in my arms,
I feel your warmth,
and I will dance until the dawn
'cos I don't want to lose you again, oh no.

And I don't want this song to ever end 'cos I know if it did then you would disappear again. Let this be forever 3 a.m., caught in a loop that repeats endlessly.

It was the mirror ball that did it – a chance reflection that sparked you back to life – like you'd just been to the bar for a little while. And you smiled and there was nothing in your eyes – not like this silt in mine making it hard to get around.

I thought you'd gone, but all this time I'd been carrying you around in my eyes. In my eyes.

You're in my eyes.

And one day my eyes will be full: a snow storm every time I shake my head. But that day is not tonight. And if we keep moving – dancing tight – they might never catch us.

I don't want to lose you again.

# Notes

## MY LIGHTHOUSE

I'd seen the Jean-Jacques Beineix film *Diva* at the cinema some time before. There was a character in the film who lived in a lighthouse, which struck me as the height of sophistication at the time.

## LITTLE GIRL (WITH BLUE EYES)

I came across a picture of my mother on her wedding day in which she looked very young and apprehensive. My mother's eyes are actually hazel.

## 97 LOVERS

*Sleeve notes*
Why 97? It could just have easily been 970 or 9,700. Just take a short walk around town and you soon lose count of the deformities. By the way, what's that growing on your back?

This was the first time I included sleeve notes on a Pulp record. I enjoy doing them because it feels like a personal aside to the people who actually buy your records rather than (at that time) taping them off the radio or (at the present time) downloading them. Just a quiet word between friends. I have included them in this section as part of the notes for the song they refer to. Album sleeve notes are included in the notes section for the first song from that particular album that wasn't released as a single.

'*I know a woman with a picture of Roger Moore in a short towelling dressing-gown*' The woman with the picture of Roger Moore on her bedroom wall was my Aunt Rita who lived just down the road from us.

## MY LEGENDARY GIRLFRIEND

This song came from improvisations. The lyrics would change from performance to performance. Over time this got formalised into a more structured arrangement but it was still semi-improvised when we got round to recording it. Hence the rather strange proclamation of 'No cheese tonight'.

'*Oh, Pitsmoor Woman*' Pitsmoor is the area of Sheffield where said girlfriend was living at the time. I was thinking of the song 'L.A. Woman' by the Doors.

## COUNTDOWN

After leaving school I was counting on my life just starting to 'happen' at some point. Then it struck me that the countdown might actually go on for ever without me ever achieving lift-off. It was realisations such as this (and the one mentioned in the next song, 'Space') that led to me leave Sheffield in September 1988 (for London – not outer space).

## SPACE

'*after days trying to sell washing machines in the rain*' My mother gave me a portable washing machine made out of orange-and-white plastic when I left home. I never used it and I attempted to sell it when I'd run out of money one week. I carried it to every shop on a street in Sheffield that was full of second-hand dealers but no one would offer me any cash for it. So I found myself standing at a bus stop, still carrying the useless thing, about to spend the last of the money I had on the ride home. Then it began to rain. I'd always imagined that I would be living on a space station or travelling to Mars by the age I was now and at that precise moment I suddenly felt, very keenly, just how far away from that situation I actually was.

## BABIES

*Sleeve notes*
Yes it happened years ago on some damp, acrylic afternoon. I know you got your own back years later (that's another story) but it wasn't such a big deal anyway – in those days you packed people rather than divorced them. I liked it that way and still do, but then again I'm imma.

'*Well it happened years ago, when you lived on Stanhope Road*' Stanhope Road is a street in Intake, the area of Sheffield in which I was brought up. It leads on to the school field of the infant and junior school I attended.

## SHEFFIELD: SEX CITY

'*Intake . . . Manor Park . . . The Wicker . . .*' These are all areas of Sheffield.

'*I was only about eleven when this happened*' This passage (spoken on the record by Candida Doyle, Pulp's keyboard player) is taken from *My Secret Garden*, a collection of women's sexual fantasies edited by Nancy Friday.

'*sophisticated lady, I wanna be your lover, not your brother or your mother, yeah*' The first example of the rhyming scheme which gives this collection its title.

'*the fares went up at seven*' Sheffield City Council's policy of providing cheap bus travel throughout South Yorkshire (a flat 2p fare for children, for example) came under pressure in the mid-1980s. At some point in 1986 a two-tier system was introduced, making travel more expensive after 7 p.m. on weekdays.

*'On a hill top at 4 a.m. the whole city is your jewellery box'* From Skye Edge you get a panoramic view of Sheffield city centre.

*'Everyone on Park Hill came in unison'* Park Hill is a large block of flats designed by Jack Lynn and Ivor Smith which opened on 16 June 1961. The flats are currently undergoing redevelopment.

*'We heard groans from a T-reg Chevette'* Pulp guitarist Mark Webber was driving a blue T-reg Vauxhall Chevette at the time.


RAZZMATAZZ

*Sleeve notes*
. . . the bits that *Hello* leaves out

*'The trouble with your brother? He's always sleeping with your mother'* The second example of the rhyming scheme that gives this collection its title.

*'Razzmatazz'* was the name of a Tyne Tees TV pop-music show that aired from 1977 to 1982.

*'looks like some bad comedian'* Rowan Atkinson

*'eating boxes of Milk Tray'* Milk Tray is a milk chocolate assortment first manufactured by Cadbury's in 1915.

*'Things go better with a little bit of razzmatazz'* A quote from the 1981 hit song of the same name by Quincy Jones.

*Sleeve notes*
The 'Story in Three Songs' follows Susan from puberty in Rotherham through wild teen years in Sheffield to her eventual marriage and settling down somewhere on the outskirts of London. I played these songs to Susan the other day – she just laughed and said I was being spiteful because she wouldn't sleep with me when we first met. She also said to tell you that she's perfectly happy where she is at the moment, thank you very much.

1   Stacks
'Stacks' means 'a lot of' in Sheffield-speak. It also refers to the stack-heeled shoes that were in fashion in the UK in the mid-1970s.

*'was he ace?'* Ace was the word used to mean 'fantastic' or 'great' when I was at secondary school.

2   Inside Susan
*'She adds up the numbers on her bus ticket to see if they make twenty-one'* It was said to denote good luck if a set of numbers added up to twenty-one: for example, ticket number 062409 would be a 'lucky' ticket. I still apply this test to any ticket I receive.

*'a man who spends all day forcing felt-tip pens into people's hands and then trying to make them pay for them'* There was a particularly enterprising beggar who used to stand outside Castle Market in Sheffield attempting to get money from passers-by using this method.

3   59, Lyndhurst Grove
I went to a party at a house with this address in the early 1990s when I was living in Camberwell, London. I hadn't been

officially invited and after a while was asked to leave by the man of the house. The song was therefore written partly as an act of revenge. The worst fate that I could imagine lying in store for Susan was to end up married to a guy like that. She, of course, may have disagreed (see the original sleeve notes).

### THE BABYSITTER

'The Babysitter' wasn't a part of 'Inside Susan – A Story in Three Songs' but is presented along with it here as it provides a postscript (of sorts) to Susan's story.

### LIPGLOSS

> *Sleeve notes*
> Welcome to the new era. Now we all live on cosmetics and garage food . . . We might look rough but we've got beautiful insides. But everything's going to be alright. Just as long as you mind the low-flying televisions.

I was thinking of the flavoured lipgloss that became available in the UK in the mid-1970s.

### STREET LITES

'*Someone wants to watch by the side of the Lina Stores*' Lina Stores is an Italian delicatessen situated at 18 Brewer Street in Soho.

### DO YOU REMEMBER THE FIRST TIME?

> *Sleeve notes*
> Well do you? And why did you choose them? Was it the drink or the time of year or the position of the planets?
>
> Or was it just their hair?

A documentary film was made to accompany the record release of this song. It explored various people's memories of losing their virginity. The film and the song came from the realisation that my own experience, which at the time had seemed so personal and private, had faded in significance enough for me to consider using it as source material. I was both appalled and intrigued by this development.

## DEEP-FRIED IN KELVIN

The lyrics refer to the Kelvin flats, a high-rise council housing estate built in the early 1960s in the Walkley district of Sheffield. They comprised a large thirteen-storey block containing about a thousand flats in total. Like the better-known Park Hill flats, the design was based around the idea of 'streets in the sky'. This was in the form of four long and very broad walkways, on to which the front doors of the flats opened.

The whole complex was demolished in the early 1990s. In the years leading up to this, the flats had become increasingly dilapidated.

I lived in a shared house just behind these flats from 1987 to 1988.

*'conceived in the toilets of Meadowhall'* Meadowhall was the largest shopping centre in Europe when it opened on 4 September 1990 on the outskirts of Sheffield.

*'A woman on the fourteenth floor noticed that her ceiling was bulging'* This is based on a real incident that occurred when an acquaintance became mentally unbalanced after being glassed in a city-centre nightclub.

*'And we drink Diamond White'* Diamond White is a cheap (and very strong) brand of cider. It was probably the first of the so-called 'alcopops' that have been blamed for the 'binge-drinking phenomenon' among young Britons.

*'In the end, the question you have to ask yourself is: are you talking to me, or are you chewing a brick?'* The answer? 'Either way, you lose your teeth.' A Sheffield threat.

JOYRIDERS

His 'n' Hers *album sleeve notes*
Please deliver us from matching sweatshirts and 'chicken in the rough', from evenings sat on couple row admiring the flock, from Sundays spent parading the aisles of Meadowhall. We don't want to live like this. It's bad for our health. Do something soon or it's curtains (just as long as they match the walls and the sofa).

Pulp used to rehearse in a room above Banks Pottery (which belonged to the mother of drummer Nick Banks) in Catcliffe, near Sheffield. By 1993 I owned a car, a yellow 1974 Hillman Imp. Once, after a rehearsal, I left on my own in the car and suddenly realised that I was about to run out of petrol. I turned the car round and headed in the direction of a garage but the car ground to a halt before I could get there. I was trying to push the car off the road so that I could make my way to the garage on foot when a new Ford Mondeo pulled up and the (very young) driver asked me what was up. His (also very young) friends got out of the back of the car and helped me push the Imp off the road. They then offered to give me a lift to the garage, which I accepted. Once inside the car I realised that it very probably did not belong to them. 'Joyriding' is a practice that began in the mid- to late 1980s in the UK. The vehicles were usually found burnt out on a housing estate the next day. The driver and his friends seemed very excited and offered me chocolate limes. We drove (at speed) to the garage and then they drove me back to my vehicle with the necessary jerrycan of fuel. This is how I repaid their kindness.

## ACRYLIC AFTERNOONS

As opposed to 'Idyllic Afternoons'.

The 'acrylic' of the title refers to the wool-like man-made fibre very popular in the clothing market in the 1950s and 1960s.

'*I had a dream about a small child in dungarees, who caught his hands in the doors of the Paris metro*' Safety signage on the Paris metro train system features a picture of a rabbit in dungarees who gets his hands trapped in the sliding doors of the carriage.

## DAVID'S LAST SUMMER

The title comes from a book called *Pennington's Last Summer* by K. M. Peyton which I spotted in my school library. I never read it.

'*Past the abandoned glasshouse stuffed full of dying palms*' Pulp once played a festival in Liverpool that was held in Sefton Park. I remember seeing a Victorian glasshouse that had been left to its own devices after public service cuts. The plants were completely overgrown and the building seemed likely to explode at any moment due to the volume of vegetation inside.

## HIS 'N' HERS

*Sleeve notes*
*His 'n' Hers* is one man's fear of domestic interiors set to music.

What are you frightened of? (And remember – shove it in sideways)

'*soap on a rope*' Once a popular Christmas gift for men. The soap doesn't get lost in the shower.

'*I'm frightened of Belgian chocolates*' Belgian chocolates were a relatively new phenomenon in 1993.

'*I'm frightened of evenings in the Brincliffe Oaks searching for a conversation*' The Brincliffe Oaks is a pub in Sheffield. I have only ever drunk there once.

During live performances of this song I tended to improvise or involve the audience in the list of phobias. Here are some examples:

> *Keele University in October 1994:*
> JARVIS: Maybe you can tell me . . . can you tell me what people in Keele are fightened of? Apart from getting crushed against that wall there. What are you frightened of?
> GIRL IN AUDIENCE: Pardon?
> JARVIS: I want to know what you're frightened of.
> GIRL: Dogs.
> JARVIS: What? Sorry.
> GIRL: Dogs!
> JARVIS: Dogs. It's not a very well-known fact . . . you've probably seen a lot of nature programmes, yeah? And in these nature programmes they make out that man was descended from the ape. And at one time we were all walking round like this, yeah? We evolved to stand upright. We evolved to stand upright and drive cars. And er . . . support football teams. But recent research . . . recent research has proved that man is not descended from the ape as had previously been believed, but man is actually descended from dogs. [. . .] This will explain a lot of behaviour you get to see at nightclubs and discos. Yeah, like a dog sniffs a lamp post . . .
>
> Butt Naked *on Channel 4, May 1994*
> JARVIS: And what makes you frightened?
> GUY IN AUDIENCE: Early evening television.

JARVIS: I know what you're saying. How about you what makes *you* frightened?

GIRL IN AUDIENCE: What makes me what? [. . .] Er, wasps.

JARVIS: Sorry?

GIRL: Wasps.

JARVIS: Wasps. Well, yeah, because they just sting people for no reason at all. If a bee stings you, it's got a reason, because it has to pay with its life, whereas wasps can just sting people for no reason at all, as many times as they want. And there are some people like that as well; in fact some people even enjoy stinging you as many times as they can. Anyway I'm getting away from the subject.

*L'Escall, Nantes, in May 1994:*

Shit! Shit, I recognise that guy, right? I saw him about ten years ago at a bus station. He was waiting for a 261 over down towards Eckington. And he was eating a bag of chips and there was all this grease going down his chin and it was kind of getting mixed up with bits of his beard. And he was wearing a kind of Pacamac kind of affair. Oh yeah, it's funny, yeah alright, but listen he's a dirty bastard . . . And then he wrapped me up in clingfilm and put some kind of white paper round me and said it looked really strong, really strong and really interesting. When in actual point of fact I looked an absolute knobhead, right. And I was unable to go out of the house for two years afterwards because people in the district where I lived took those kind of things very seriously.

Anyway, I'm digressing . . .

We were laid in bed afterwards and she asked me what frightened me.

I said: 'That's quite a personal question.'

She said: 'I know.'

I said: 'OK, I don't mind you asking me then.'

*Sleeve notes*
There is a war in progress – don't be a casual(ty). The time to decide whose side you're on is here. Choose wisely. Stay alive in '95.

During the first two weeks of my second term at St Martin's I, like all other students, had to do something called 'Crossover', where you studied a discipline other than the one you were taking a degree in. I chose sculpture, and it was during this time that I met the girl who inspired this song. Therefore she was *not* studying sculpture at St Martin's College – she was, like me, just trying it out for a couple of weeks. I never knew her name.

*'She studied sculpture at St Martin's College'* St Martin's School of Art was situated on Charing Cross Road, London, from 1854 until 2011, when it moved to a new building in King's Cross.


SORTED FOR E'S & WIZZ

*Sleeve notes*
The summer of '89: Centreforce FM, Santa Pod, Sunrise 5000, 'Ecstasy Airport', ride the white horse, the strings of life, dancing at motorway service stations, falling asleep at the wheel on the way home. There's so many people – it's got to mean something, it needs to mean something, surely it must mean something. It didn't mean nothing.

I got talking to a girl after a Pulp concert and she told me how she had been at the Stone Roses' legendary Spike Island concert but that all she could remember about the experience was lots of suspicious-looking guys wandering around asking whether everyone was 'sorted for E's & Wizz'. The phrase stuck in my mind.

*'E's'* The drug Ecstasy.

'*Wizz*' Slang for amphetamine sulphate.

'*got the tickets from some fucked-up bloke in Camden Town*'
The first rave I went to was Sunrise 5000 which was held on
20 May 1989. We had heard it advertised on Centreforce FM
(a pirate radio station) and had to go to a flat on Kentish Town
Road to buy the tickets.

'*I seem to have left an important part of my brain somewhere
in a field in Hampshire*' Sunrise 5000 was held at the Santa Pod
drag-racing facility on a disused airfield in Northamptonshire
(oops).


MIS-SHAPES

*Sleeve notes*
We shall fight them in 'The Beeches' – and 'The Stag'
and 'The King's Head' if it comes to that. You know
the score – ten blokes with 'taches in short-sleeved
white shirts telling you that you're the weirdo. Fear not
brothers and sisters – we shall prevail. Live on.

The sweet shop on the road in front of the house I was brought
up in used to sell bags of 'mis-shapes': chocolates deemed not
fit to be put in boxes due to their imperfect appearance and so
sold off at a discount.

'*raised on a diet of broken biscuits*' The biscuit equivalent of
'mis-shape' chocolates.

'*Check your lucky numbers*' The first UK National Lottery
draw was held on 19 November 1994.


I SPY

Different Class *album sleeve notes*
Please understand. We don't want no trouble. We just
want the right to be different. That's all.

'*Imagining a blue plaque above the place I first ever touched a girl's chest*' The world's first blue plaques were erected in London, England, in the nineteenth century to mark the homes and workplaces of famous people. This original scheme still survives today and is administered by English Heritage.

'*Take your* Year in Provence *and shove it up your ass*' A Year in Provence is the title of a best-selling autobiographical novel by Peter Mayle published in 1989. I have never read it.

F.E.E.L.I.N.G.C.A.L.L.E.D.L.O.V.E.

'*Just like a modern shopping centre*' The homogenisation of Britain's high streets had just begun in earnest.

DISCO 2000

The year 2000 seemed to be a significant date in all the science- fiction books, comics and films I was exposed to as a child. By then we would be living in 'The Future'. The thought of actually being alive when it came around was mind-boggling.

'*Your name is Deborah*' I was born in Nether Edge hospital, Sheffield on 19 September 1963. The woman in the bed next to my mother gave birth to a daughter a few hours later. The girl was christened Deborah Farnell and we were in the same class all the way through school.

'*with woodchip on the wall*' Woodchip is a very cheap form of wallpaper.

'*Be there two o'clock by the fountain down the road*' The Goodwin fountain at the top of the Fargate pedestrian precinct in Sheffield was a popular meeting place. Unfortunately it was demolished in 1998.

## SOMETHING CHANGED

*'I wrote this song two hours before we met'* I did in fact write the music for this song twelve years before it was recorded so that gave me the idea for the conceit of the lyrics.

## LIVE BED SHOW

When I left Sheffield to move to London in 1988 I bought a bed from the Salvation Army furniture store to take down with me, as I was going to be living in a squat. It did indeed cost £10. A few years later I moved into a furnished flat and lent the bed to a friend. When I finally bought my own house in 1997 the bed was returned to me and I couldn't help but wonder about what events had taken place on it in the interim.

## BAR ITALIA

Lou and Caterina Polledri first opened Bar Italia at 22 Frith Street, Soho in 1949. The cafe is open twenty-four hours a day, so it is a popular stopping-off point before people try to get home after a night out.

## MILE END

Mile End is in the borough of Tower Hamlets, East London.

*'I know this place off Burdett Road'* Having been evicted from our squat in Camberwell we moved into Lewey House, a tower block in E3.

*'and maybe shoot somebody if they lose at pool'* This is true: the incident was reported in the local paper.

*'The pearly king of the Isle of Dogs feels up children in the bogs'* This is not true. I don't even know if there is a pearly king of the Isle of Dogs.

The title came from a song by The Goodies called 'Cricklewood Shakedown'. The Goodies were a popular comedy trio in the UK in the mid-1970s.

Catcliffe is a village just outside Rotherham. The pottery warehouse where Pulp used to rehearse was there.

*'it's a fare and a half'* Sheffield taxi drivers charged extra to drive there as it was beyond the city limits.

*'Pudgy twelve-year-olds in Union Jack shorts addicted to coffee-whitener and frankfurters'* This image appeared in two unreleased songs (this one and 'Modern Marriage') before finally making it on record as part of 'Wickerman', from the 2001 album *We Love Life*.

*'Mister, we just want your car'* A quote from 'Joyriders'.

*'a meal in a glass'* Guinness is sometimes referred to in this way.

*'they were going to open an airport'* Catcliffe did indeed become home to Sheffield City Airport which opened in 1997 – and closed in 2002.

*'duty-free parkin'* Parkin is a heavy ginger cake usually eaten around the time of Guy Fawkes night.

*'amongst the Airfix planes'* Airfix have been manufacturing plastic construction kits since 1952.

*'the dismembered remains of Matchstalk Men and Matchstalk Cats and Dogs'* 'Matchstalk Men and Matchstalk Cats and Dogs' was a number-one single for the duo Brian and Michael in 1978. The song told the life story of the artist L. S. Lowry and the pair performed it on television dressed in flat caps and clogs, accompanied by a children's choir.

*'Panda Pops'* Low-priced fizzy drinks produced between 1975 and 2011.

*'stunted by vapours from the cooling towers'* Tinsley cooling towers were demolished on 24 August 2008.


P.T.A (PARENT TEACHER ASSOCIATION)

*'I was too scared to touch the girls at the Poly'* Polytechnics were vocation-based higher education establishments. They usually accepted entrants with lower grades. They were abolished in 1992 and formally rebranded as universities – presumably to boost government figures listing university graduates.


SET THE CONTROLS FOR THE HEART OF THE PELVIS

This song featured on the Barry Adamson album *Oedipus Schmoedipus*. Barry also provided the song's title.


COCAINE SOCIALISM

The meeting depicted in the song is fictional but I was invited to a number of Labour Party functions in the lead-up to the 1997 UK election. Cocaine Socialism seemed the next logical step after Champagne Socialism. Pulp recorded the song just before I embarked upon an ill-advised trip to New York around Christmas 1996. I was supposed to be travelling incognito but was called at the hotel I was staying at by an 'Imogen from New Labour' who wanted to know, 'Can we count on your support?' This made me incredibly paranoid and probably contributed to the nervous collapse I suffered soon after.

New Labour won the 1997 election.


GLORY DAYS

After I returned from New York, the 1997 election came and went while I was prevaricating over what to do with 'Cocaine

Socialism'. The song eventually got 'recycled' as 'Glory Days' and was released on the *This Is Hardcore* album in 1998.

*'learn the meaning of existence in fortnightly instalments'* Giro cheques for those on Unemployment Benefit or Social Security were posted once every two weeks.

*'I used to do the* I Ching*'* Chinese fortune-telling involving the use of three coins.

*'I could do anything if I could get a Round Tuit'* Round Tuits were sold as seaside novelties. If you received one, you no longer had an excuse to put off a boring chore (e.g. 'When are you going to put that shelf up?', 'When I get around to it.')


HELP THE AGED

> *Sleeve notes*
> So do you expect us to start drinking Port & Lemon all of a sudden? The Rave is on. Leave your wheelchair outside.

Help the Aged is a UK charity (now called Age UK) set up to aid elderly people. It has many charity shops across the country.


THIS IS HARDCORE

> *Sleeve notes*
> Taking it all the way down the marrowbone. Hold tight.
>
> Now is the time of the quickening. By the way – that goes in there.

All I had for this song was the title. I sat down to write the lyrics and got so drunk that I couldn't remember having written them when I woke up the next morning. I applied the same method to recording the vocal. I don't know how much I believe in the id but those words came from somewhere.

'*That goes in there*' Hardcore porn movies have very strict conventions: all orifices must be seen to be penetrated and the male's ejaculation must also be visible. It reminds me of dinosaur movies: if you watch any film featuring prehistoric creatures made between the 1950s and the 1980s, you can be sure that once a T. Rex has entered the scene then a Triceratops will not be far behind it, and they will proceed to conduct a fight to the death.

## THE PROFESSIONAL

'*Psychic karaoke every weekend*' One effect of panic attacks and psychosis can be that you get the feeling that you are performing the act of being you. In effect, being a 'cover version' of yourself.

## LAUGHING BOY

I ended up with a houseguest from Iceland who overstayed his welcome. He became known as 'Laughing Boy'.

## THE FEAR

> This Is Hardcore *album sleeve notes*
> It's OK to grow up – just as long as you don't grow old.
> Face it . . . you are young.

'*This is our "Music From a Bachelor's Den"*' Music For A Bachelor's Den was a series of 'lounge music' compilations released in the early 1990s.

'*You're gonna like it – but not a lot*' Paul Daniels is a famous English magician who appeared many times on TV in the 1980s and 1990s. His catch-phrase was 'You'll like it – not a lot – but you'll like it'.

*'A man told me to beware of thirty-three'* Just before my thirty-third birthday someone cornered me at a party and told me all about 'The Christ Age' and how lots of men were supposed to have mid-life crises when they measured their achievements against those of Jesus (who was crucified at the age of thirty-three).

## PARTY HARD

Pulp played a pretty horrendous corporate event in Barcelona in August 1996. In the run-up to the concert one of the organisers informed us that he liked to party 'pretty fucking hard'.

## TV MOVIE

In the 1970s UK TV listings used the phrase 'made for TV' to denote imported American 'tele-movies'. The American broadcasting laws of the time meant that these films contained no profane language or nudity and so were of no interest whatsoever to my teenage self.

*'and there's nothing on TV'* In those days TV stations went off air after a certain time at night and broadcast the test card.

## A LITTLE SOUL

My housemate's father died suddenly and it made me think about my own father, who had left home when I was seven years old and whom I had not seen since apart from a brief visit when I was twelve.

## MODERN MARRIAGE

This was an attempt to imagine a new set of wedding vows

more suited to the modern age. I was engaged at the time but the marriage never took place.

'*And what if our kids turn into pudgy blobs*' This was the second appearance of this image, the first being in 'Catcliffe Shakedown'. It finally featured on an official release in 'Wickerman' (2001).

'*Oh yeah, I'm shitting Barratt houses here*' To 'shit bricks' is a South Yorkshire expression meaning to be 'very scared'. The protagonist is so scared that he is shitting entire houses; Barratt Homes is a well-known UK construction company.


FIRST MAN IN SPACE

A song from the album *Pickled Eggs & Sherbet* by All Seeing-I, for which I wrote several lyrics. This one was sung by Phil Oakey, the lead singer of Sheffield electronic band The Human League, which was formed in 1977 and achieved worldwide fame with their 1981 album *Dare*.

'*I threw away my packing up*' Packed lunch.

'*bones that have crumbled to dust*' Prolonged periods of weightlessness lead to brittle bones.

'*how're you supposed to open these new milk cartons?*' Tetra-pak milk cartons were superseded by screw-top plastic 'flagons' during the late 1990s.

'*Why don't they make Golden Nuggets no more?*' Golden Nuggets were a breakfast cereal, popular in my childhood, made by Nabisco. Production was halted in the late 1970s but was revived in 1999.

'*Lumps of rock*' See the earlier lyric for 'Space'.

'*Parties with no atmosphere*' 'Atmosphere' was a no. 7 hit for Russ Abbott in 1984.

This song was sung by Tony Christie on the All Seeing-I album. Christie was born in Conisborough, South Yorkshire, and became a famous cabaret singer in the early 1970s. I had a copy of a magazine called *Easy Listening* from the period of Tony's first rise to fame which featured an 'at home' interview with him. Elsewhere in the same magazine was an article about the TV show *Stars on Sunday*. This was a religious programme that aired on the independent TV network between 1969 and 1979. It featured religious music and celebrities discussing their faith.

*'they were sold off to Patnicks'* A large junk shop on London Road in Sheffield. Irvine Patnick, the owner, was a Tory councillor.

*'balling the jack in a granny flat'* 'Balling the Jack' is a song written by Jim Burris and Chris Smith, first published in 1913. Very popular at pensioner sing-alongs.

*'The chicken has flown the basket'* Chicken in a basket was a staple of the menus of the cabaret clubs that flourished for a while in the early 1970s.

### THE QUIET REVOLUTION

This song has never been officially released. At one point I intended it to be the title track of the next Pulp album, but the singer-songwriter Chris de Burgh released an album of the same name in 1999 and I abandoned the idea (and the song).

*'You could have heard a pin drop at Gatecrasher last Thursday at 4 a.m.'* Gatecrasher was a very popular dance club in Sheffield in the late 1990s and early 2000s.

*'I've seen how the world ends, and it's not with a bang but a*

*whisper'* Paraphrasing the last line of T. S. Eliot's 'The Hollow Men'.

WEEDS II (THE ORIGIN OF THE SPECIES)

The song's title quotes (incorrectly) Charles Darwin's landmark work.

*'drinking Nurishment'* Nurishment is a milk-based energy drink available in many UK newsagents.

*'a sensational buzz – zzzzzz'* 'Sensational Buzz' is the title of a 1979 B-side by the group Racey.

WICKERMAN

The starting point for this lyric was a piece I wrote for *World of Interiors* in January 2000. This is the piece in full:

> *Acrylic Afternoons* by Jarvis Cocker
> The River Porter is visible at the side of Sheffield's train station. It runs through a concrete channel for about twenty yards before disappearing into a tunnel. Sometime in the mid-eighties, myself and some friends decided to follow the river as far as possible. At first we attempted to stay out of the water as it appeared very polluted: large, oily globules the colour of ketchup covered the surface. This soon proved impossible and we waded through the knee-high water, hoping not to contract an industrial disease. Sometimes the river would run through a dirty brickwork tunnel for a quarter of a mile or so (which was quite scary, seeing as no one had thought to bring a torch) and then it would emerge in another part of town – never where we expected. It seemed quite amazing to discover such an adventure in the middle of the city we had grown up in and which we all professed to be totally bored with.

I suppose this discovery must have given me a taste for river exploration, as next year I attempted to navigate Sheffield's largest river, the Don. This flows mostly above ground, though it has many weirs along its length which make it slightly treacherous. I had purchased an inflatable dinghy from a jumble sale, so this trip had an altogether more official air about it. I was living in an old warehouse in an area known as the Wicker and the river flowed directly past. One summer afternoon, myself and a friend blew up the boat and set off on our adventure. And an adventure it was.

After a couple of close calls with weirs, we began to relax and enjoy our journey. We were travelling downstream so we didn't have to do much rowing, and somehow drifting past familiar landmarks from a different angle seemed to fill us with excitement. At one point we were enveloped in steam from a neighbouring factory and I began to have a feeling that maybe we were involved in some kind of South Yorkshire re-creation of *Apocalypse Now* – it was like the river had decided where it wanted to take us.

The journey continued and the landscape began to get less familiar. We saw some gypsy kids using a bread crate to kind of 'sledge' down a weir. Some parts of the river were almost stagnant, with large, evil-smelling bubbles rising to the surface. We had seen quite a few fishermen along the route, but, as we approached Rotherham, we came across a man attempting to shoot fish with an air rifle – whilst uttering the immortal words 'Stitch that, you bastards!' Maybe this scared us slightly; anyway, soon after that we deflated the boat and got the bus home but not before marking our end point with a pile of stones and vowing to finish our journey at a later date. Of course, this never happened and the boat got punctured in a later incident but that day has stuck in my mind as one of the happiest of my life, so I couldn't entirely rule out going back to continue it one day – even this long after the event.

*'Just behind the station before you reach the traffic island'* This describes the location of the River Porter. It is quite accurate geographically.

*'I think it was after the Leadmill'* The Leadmill is an old Sheffield bus garage that opened as a music venue in 1980. Pulp's first-ever Sheffield performance took place there on 16 August 1980 as part of a local bands' festival called Bouquet of Steel.

*'connecting white witches on the Moor, with Pre-Raphaelites down in Broomhall'* The Moor is a pedestrianised shopping precinct in the centre of town. Broomhall is a down-at-heel area near the University.

*'Beneath the old Trebor factory'* The sweet factory was actually on the outskirts of Chesterfield and closed in March 2005.

*'caverns of nougat and caramel'* I was fascinated by the way 'nougat' was pronounced in the TV adverts of my childhood: 'noo-gar' rather than 'nuh-gut'.

*'the river flows on beneath pudgy fifteen-year-olds addicted to coffee-whitener'* Finally! (See notes for 'Catcliffe Shakedown' and 'Modern Marriage'.)

*'courting couples naked on Northern Upholstery'* Northern Upholstery was a furniture retailer with outlets in Brigg, Thorpe Arch and Wetherby. It was rebranded as DFS in the mid-1990s.

*'it finally comes above ground again at Forge Dam'* The cafe mentioned in the song was still open for business at the time of writing these notes.

*'At the other end of town the river flows underneath an old railway viaduct'* This is Conisborough viaduct (see the *World of Interiors* article for details).

'*in a disused factory just off the Wicker*' The Wicker is a major road in Sheffield city centre. I lived in a caretaker's flat, above a disused factory that had been converted into music rehearsal rooms and light industrial units, on Sheldon Row, just off it, from 1983 to 1985.

## BAD COVER VERSION

'*Bikini-clad girl on the front who invited you in*' The Pickwick record label specialised in cheap 'Top of the Pops' albums which featured cover versions of current hits performed in the style of the original artists. The record sleeves always featured a photo of a scantily-clad glamour model in a seductive pose.

'*when it's electronically reprocessed – to give a more life-like effect*' Other record labels, such as Camden, repackaged old hits from the 1950s and 1960s in modern, colourful sleeves. As many of the tracks featured were originally recorded in mono they were often 'electronically reprocessed to give a stereo effect'. Usually with disastrous results.

'*last days of Southfork*' Southfork was the name of the ranch in the American TV series *Dallas*.

'*the second side of* "Til the Band Comes In' '*Til the Band Comes In* is Scott Walker's fifth solo LP (released in 1970). It is an unusual record in that it starts off with eight high-quality original compositions and then concludes with six very bland cover versions of standards. As a fan this seemed to be the sound of someone 'throwing in the towel' halfway through the recording process. This line led to an embarassing situation as, after a number of false starts, Pulp ended up recording *We Love Life* (which features 'Bad Cover Version') with Scott Walker as record producer. It was coming close to the day when I was going to have to record my vocal for the track and I was really trying to find the right moment to broach the subject of the song's lyrics with him, but it never seemed to come along. Then one morning as I was travelling to the studio on the train I resolved to tell him about it as soon as I walked through the door, to get it out of the way. So I got off the train, walked into the studio, pinned him up against the mixing desk and just blurted it out. At first he just looked at me in a bemused fashion and then it seemed to dawn on him what I was babbling about; he laughed and said, 'Well, gee thanks – that's the way you repay all my hard work.' It later transpired that he doesn't actually own any of his old records so I think he'd forgotten that he'd made that one. But for me, it was mortifying.

## THE LAST DAY OF THE MINERS' STRIKE

The miners' strike was an industrial dispute that took place between 1984 and 1985. It is generally considered to be the moment that the Conservative government (led by Margaret Thatcher) 'broke' the Trade Union movement in the UK. One of the most famous incidents in the strike was the so-called 'Battle of Orgreave' which took place on 18 June 1984. It was basically a pitched battle between the striking miners and the police force. I had been on a school trip to the coke-smelting plant at Orgreave as a child and the Pulp rehearsal room at Catcliffe was within walking distance of the site of the conflict.

*'seems the last day of the miners' strike was the Magna Carta in this part of town'* In 1215 the Magna Carta was the first document forced on to an English king by a group of his subjects, the feudal barons, in an attempt to limit his powers by law and protect their privileges.

*'Some joker in a headband was still getting chicks for free'* Mark Knopfler of Dire Straits. Dire Straits released a song called 'Iron Hand' which referred to Orgreave.

Relaxed Muscle was a fictional band I formed with my friend Jason Buckle after Pulp took a break in 2002. The idea was that we were a 'Techno-Billy' duo from Doncaster (Jason's home town). I sang under the pseudonym of Darren Spooner, a former club-singer going through a messy divorce and with a drinking problem. This subterfuge was maintained for the band's first release (the 'Heavy EP') but our cover was blown after our first public appearance at Bethnal Green Working Men's Club in May 2003 (even though I was heavily disguised and spoke through a voice-altering effects unit). *A Heavy Nite With Relaxed Muscle*, released in October 2003, was the band's only album.

To provide further insight into the Relaxed Muscle ethos I have included this piece which first appeared in the Christmas 2003 edition of London's *Time Out* listings magazine.

*Darren's Dream*

It was night-time and I was outside on a country road. There were hundreds of toads trying to cross the road to get to their mating pond but they were moving too slowly and were getting squashed by passing juggernauts. I wanted to pick them up and carry them across the road to the pond, but I didn't have anything to put them in and I don't like touching things that are slimy.

Suddenly I was standing on some cellar steps with a bad stomach-ache. There was an awful taste in my mouth. I realised that I had swallowed the toads in order to transport them. I began heaving and eventually sicked up a large toad covered in thick mucus. Then another. Then another. After a while a door opened at the top of the cellar steps and someone shouted down my name. Barry White was due on stage in ten minutes and I hadn't ironed his shirt yet. I ran up the stairs and I was in the kitchen area of the Park and Abourthorne

Working Men's Club. An ironing board was set up near the cooker with Barry's shirt on it but I couldn't plug the iron in 'cos it had a European plug on it and the power point was English. Jane Seymour walked into the room wearing the same outfit as in *Sinbad and the Eye of the Tiger*. She put her arms around my shoulders and tried to kiss me. I said I had to finish the shirt. 'How do you think I got my hair so straight?' she said. She took the plug of the iron and put it in her mouth, then she bent over the ironing board and began ironing the shirt. I took her from behind as she was doing this and the iron let out a cloud of steam. Soon it was like a sauna. Her skin was smooth and covered in beads of sweat. I felt that I was about to come. I closed my eyes in order to savour the moment.

In my ear I heard the words, 'Is everybody in? Is everybody in?' I opened my eyes and I was sat around a campfire with some Red Indians. Jim Morrison was dancing and singing with a bottle of Newcastle Brown in his hand, which he kept swigging from. He had a long beard and was very overweight. He was wearing a flowery shirt and tracksuit bottoms. The smoke from the fire was burning my eyes. I looked down and saw I still had a hard-on. None of the Indians had noticed. They were arguing about whether to allow a monster truck rally that was scheduled to take place on their land the next day to go ahead. Jim began to sing 'I Believe I Can Fly'. The Indians took no notice. I was appalled because he was getting all the words wrong.

A shot rang out. Jim fell on to the fire and was immediately engulfed in flames. He burnt blue like when you put rum on a Christmas pudding. 'I guess that's all the alcohol,' I thought. Charles Bronson approached the campfire, his rifle still smoking. He was dressed like in *Chato's Land* (my favourite film). He offered me some chips. 'They're cooked in dog fat,' he said. I took one to be polite. The toad taste came back into my mouth and I had to spit. It landed on one of Bronson's moccasins. The Indians went crazy and dragged me to my feet. Bronson was laughing. They dragged me over to a large wooden pole stuck in the ground. Eva Herzigova was already tied to it wearing her bra and pants, like in those adverts from a few years ago. They tied me up so that my body was against hers, face to face. 'Save me, save me,' she whispered. Her breath was hot on my cheek. I wanted to do it to her, but I was tied so tight I couldn't move. I knew that in a few seconds we were going to be burnt at the stake. All I could do was rub myself against her a bit. As I rubbed she kept whispering, 'Save me, save me', and the pole began to grow out of the ground, going higher and higher and higher. 'The flames will never reach us here,' she said and we started kissing. Suddenly there was the sound of a gunshot and her body went limp. Bronson was shooting from below. The same shot that had killed her had broken the ropes holding me. I moved round to the other side of the pole and began shinning up it. At the top of the pole was a trapdoor. I pushed it open and climbed through.

I found myself in a Shaolin temple, just like the one at the end of *Enter the Dragon*. Bruce Lee was sitting on the floor crying. I asked him what was wrong. He told me that his manager had signed a sponsorship deal with Gap and now he had to wear cargo pants whenever he fought plus he was signed up to do a tour of British holiday camps during the summer demonstrating his martial arts skills. I saw that he was indeed wearing cargo pants although they were black instead of the usual khaki colour. I told him from a distance no one would be able to tell. This seemed to enrage him and he jumped up into a fighting pose. I said I didn't want to fight because he was one of my heroes, but he wouldn't back off. He kept doing flying kicks to my face, but I wouldn't fight back. My nose started bleeding and when I looked down there was a Yorkshire terrier licking up the pool of blood that had collected at my feet. I kicked at it to shoo it away and it sunk its teeth into my foot. It didn't really hurt, just like little pins sticking in me, but it was irritating. I tried to shake him off but he wouldn't let go. I kicked him against the wall but he still wouldn't let go. I realised that I was going to have to beat the dog to death to get it off my foot. I didn't want to do this because I'm an animal lover so I started to cry. Then I heard Bruce Lee laughing at me and I lost my temper. I gave him a roundhouse kick to the head. He fell to the floor and when he got up the Yorkshire terrier was attached to his face. It seemed to be eating his cheek. He screamed and jumped through one of those paper screens they always have in Kung Fu films.

I looked at my watch and saw that it was half-past eleven. I suddenly remembered that we were supposed to be playing a concert and that we were due on stage at eleven fifteen. I was late! I pushed open the temple doors and I could hear music coming from up a staircase. I ran up the stairs and I was under the stage. The stage was see-through and I could see the rest of the band playing without me. I banged on the stage but they couldn't hear me 'cos they always play so bloody loud. (It was like that bit where the kid's under the ice in *The Omen*.) They finished the song and I managed to attract Jason's attention. He opened a trapdoor and I was on stage, then he started laughing. I looked down and I still had a hard-on and no trousers.

Then I woke up.

*'I saw it on* Later*, so I got the CD'* Later with Jools Holland *is a BBC TV music programme that first aired on 9 October 1992.*

*'DJs, late bar, stone-baked pizza'* The slogan of a bar/restaurant just around the corner from Angel tube station in London.

### MARY

Mary is Darren's estranged wife.

*'Last night I saw Darren, he didn't recognise me – he offered me out'* Darren's son is also called Darren.

### SLIDING THROUGH LIFE ON CHARM

Pulp performed on the Channel Four TV show *TFI Friday* on 11 September 1998 to promote the single 'Party Hard'. Metallica performed on the same show and Marianne Faithfull was singing with them. I had a conversation with her later during which she suggested that I write a song for her. I said that I would be happy to do this provided she came up with a title first to get the ball rolling. She came up with the title on the spot – the song took considerably longer. It was delivered too late for inclusion on her 1999 album *Vagabond Days* and so ended up on *Kissin' Time*, released in 2002.

*'Now everybody wants to kiss my snatch'* A reference to 'Why'd Ya Do It?' from Marianne's album *Broken English*.

*'I never got any royalties'* Most of the biographical information in the song was gleaned from *Faithfull*, a memoir published in 1994.

### THE OPERATION

Through a peculiar set of circumstances I happened to walk into a Parisian studio where Charlotte Gainsbourg and the French duo Air were making an album together. On the night of my visit they were all sitting around a microphone, having a conversation in an attempt to generate some ideas/material for song lyrics. I had the feeling that my presence wasn't really helping the process. About a week later the man producing the album, Nigel Godrich, called and asked if I'd be interested in writing some lyrics for the project.

Writing for Charlotte was a far more collaborative experience than the song for Marianne had been. I was in the studio whilst the music was being worked on and I would show Charlotte my lyrical ideas. 'The Operation' started out as a fairly romantic song about a lover trying to atone for his past sins by mending his former lover's heart. Charlotte found this idea too 'soppy' and suggested the story take a darker route. I followed her suggestions and the song improved immeasurably as a result.

SET YOURSELF ON FIRE

Towards the end of the Charlotte Gainsbourg/Air album there were a series of riots on the outskirts of Paris (the first I heard of it was when a friend from London called to tell me they'd seen it on the TV news). For a few weeks the trouble threatened to spread into the centre of town.

'*Coffee at the Flore*' The Cafe de Flore is a cafe on Boulevard Saint-Germain, Paris. It was a favourite meeting place for members of the Existentialist movement in the 1950s and continues to host intellectual events.

CUNTS ARE STILL RUNNING THE WORLD

I was queueing in a bank on holiday when the title for this song popped into my head. I finally got round to recording a demo version of it on the night of the Live 8 event on 2 July 2005, which I had been watching all day. Exactly one year later the song became my introduction to the world of 'social media' when it formed the basis of my MySpace page – a convenient way of introducing a track with un-broadcastable lyrical content into the public domain. The welcome page to the site read thus:

> If all the technical bits and pieces are working properly then you should be able to hear a new song I've been working on. I wanted you to hear it now 'cos it's exactly one year since that Live 8 thing and it was the night of that event that I wrote this song. I apologise for all the swearing but sometimes that's the only thing that seems appropriate. It's in no way a criticism of Geldof & co. but I remember thinking at the time: 'Where does engaging with these politicians/businessmen really get you?' (twelve months on and the cunts still haven't paid up as far as I can make out) maybe the problem is something more . . . fundamental. Anyway, what do I know? I'm just a pampered rock star – but at least I think it's good to discuss this stuff. Don't you? Let me know what you think.

*'Find a school near the top of the league'* School league tables were first published in the UK in 1994, inevitably leading to greater inequalities in the publicly funded education system.

*'use your right to protest on the street'* The march against the Iraq war on 15 February 2003 was the largest public demonstration ever to take place in the UK. It failed to prevent the invasion.

DISNEY TIME

*Disney Time* was a BBC TV show broadcast on or around public holidays between 1970 and 1984. It consisted of excerpts from famous Walt Disney productions, such as *Mary Poppins* and *Bedknobs and Broomsticks*. This was considered a rare treat at the time, as Disney films were never shown in their entirety on British terrestrial TV during this period.

Although the intro is an abridged version of the opening para-
graph of Carson McCullers' *The Member of the Wedding*,
much of the song's lyrics are freely borrowed from *The Heart
is a Lonely Hunter*, in particular the lines:

> In the quiet, secret light she was by herself again. It was
> not late – yellow squares of light showed in the windows
> of the houses along the streets. She walked slow, with her
> hands in her pockets and her head to one side. (Penguin
> Modern Classics reprint 2008, page 106)

The book partly explores the world of a fourteen-year-old girl
called Mick Kelly, who is an outsider, atheist and dreamer.
In this excerpt, she hides in a neighbour's garden and listens
to a broadcast of Beethoven's Symphony No. 9 on the radio.
The music transforms her: 'It didn't have anything to do with
God.' The passage struck me as being the best description of
the experience of listening to music that I'd ever come across
in print.

*'and the Sunday-school teacher who said she had beautiful
breasts'* This came from a story told to me by a female friend
from Loughborough.

## I WILL KILL AGAIN

Peter Sutcliffe (aka The Yorkshire Ripper) murdered thirteen
women in the north of England between 1975 and 1980.
The police investigation (which eventually led to his arrest
in Sheffield on 2 January 1981) was massively side-tracked
by a character who came to be known as 'Wearside Jack'.
The police received a cassette tape purporting to be from the
killer on 17 June 1979. It was broadcast on the national news
media in the hope that someone would recognise the voice and
come forward with fresh information as to the killer's identity.

The voice on the tape had a thick Geordie accent (hence the nickname) and certain phrases passed into popular parlance, 'I will kill again' being one of them. It came to signify a willingness to 'go the whole hog' whatever the consequences.

Wearside Jack's identity became public in 2005. John Humble was arrested and charged with perverting the course of justice. He received a sentence of eight years.

FAT CHILDREN

*'putting bullets in some guy's head for no particular reason'*
Jean Charles de Menezes (7 January 1978–22 July 2005) was a Brazilian man shot in the head seven times at Stockwell Tube station on the London Underground by the London Metropolitan Police, after he was misidentified as one of the fugitives involved in the previous day's failed bombing attempts.

THE LOSS ADJUSTER

*'Sitting in The World's End with some indie friends'* The World's End is a pub in Camden, London. Pulp played at the Underworld, the venue beneath it, on a number of occasions.

*'The guys from Arlington House are marauding the streets'* Arlington House is a hostel for the homeless on Arlington Road in Camden.

*'And then you find yourself thinking about Egyptian Sue'* There was a girl in Sheffield during my formative years who was known as Egyptian Sue. She never indulged in any of the activities depicted in the song, though.

*'the levels of hysteria around the Kentish Town Road'* The north end of Camden.

*'a punctured Spacehopper from under some rubble in a skip'* Spacehoppers were an orange bouncing toy you could sit on.

They became a very lazy form of visual shorthand whenever an art director wished to evoke a 1970s atmosphere. I had one myself. A skip is what Americans would call a dumpster.

*'and each time you rang it was like an Indian call centre on the line'* Some time during the 2000s it became standard practice to employ call centres based in India to deal with UK bank enquiries and other customer services. They would often also cold-call regarding double-glazing or mobile-phone offers.

*'You never did see* Dog Day Afternoon' *Dog Day Afternoon* is a 1975 film directed by Sidney Lumet, starring Al Pacino. I still haven't seen it.


## FUCKINGSONG

In the animal kingdom all singing is a form of sexual display designed to attract a mate. This obviously creates certain problems for the married lead singer. Here, the solution proposed is that the song does all the fucking on the singer's behalf.


## I NEVER SAID I WAS DEEP

I may have this phrase inscribed on my tombstone.


## LEFTOVERS

The title of this song was inspired by the William H. Gass short story, 'In the Heart of the Heart of the Country'.

*'I met her in the Museum of Palaeontology'* The museum is situated in the Jardin des Plantes in Paris.

*'And now I've told you twice, Homes'* As in 'Home-Boy'. I first heard this usage in the film *Colors*.

*'The train was leaving in ten minutes or so'* I lost my son (who was six years old at the time) in St Pancras International train station. In the minutes that passed before I found him again several nightmare scenarios played themselves out in my mind.

*'Kittens are cute but a full-grown cat can be cuter'* On the Paris Metro I'd seen a woman and her retarded teenage daughter, who was playing with a teddy bear. You constantly exhort kids to 'hold still' but if they really did it would be grotesque.

## YOU'RE IN MY EYES (DISCOSONG)

*'Grey floaters inside my eyes'* Grey floaters is the medical term for flakes of skin that have become detached from the retina and then float around in the vitreous humour inside the eyeball. They are visible when you look at a featureless object such as a blank wall or a clear blue sky. As a child I was convinced that I had worms inside my eyes and was frightened to tell my mother in case I had to have a painful operation. I was going to call the song 'Grey Floaters' but friends said the title was open to misinterpretation.

*'you look real good in your halter-top'* A quote from a half-remembered disco song lyric.

*'caught in a loop that repeats endlessly'* The song is based around a looped sample.

*'a snow storm every time I shake my head'* Like one of those snow-globes you can buy at the seaside.

*'Dancing tight'* was a hit for Phil Fearon and Galaxy in 1983.

Thank you for your attention.

# Acknowledgements

Many thanks to Lee, Hannah, Kate and all at Faber for believing in this book.

I am helped on a daily basis by the stupendous Jeannette Lee plus Jessica, Kelly, Geoff Travis and the rest of Rough Trade.

Jeannette Lee and Kevin Conroy-Scott are my very capable literary agents.

The Pulp Wiki website (www.pulpwiki.net) was an invaluable source of information whilst I was compiling this book.

Thanks to Raina Lampkins-Fielder for her help with the initial selection of lyrics.

Some of the ideas included in the introduction came from a lecture called 'Saying the Unsayable' which I first presented at the Brighton Festival in 2008.

And finally, I must thank all the people who have made music with me over the years as none of these words would exist were it not for the songs that we created together.

# Copyright

'59, Lyndhurst Grove'
'A Little Soul'
'Acrylic Afternoons'
'Babies'
'Bad Cover Version'
'Bar Italia'
'Catcliffe Shakedown'
'Common People'
'David's Last Summer'
'Deep-Fried in Kelvin'
'Disco 2000'
'Dishes'
'Do You Remember the First Time?'
'F.E.E.L.I.N.G.C.A.L.L.E.D.L.O.V.E.'
'Help the Aged'
'His 'n' Hers'
'I Spy'
'Inside Susan'
'Joyriders'
'Laughing Boy'
'Lipgloss'
'Live Bed Show'
'Mile End'
'Mis-Shapes'
'Modern Marriage'
'Party Hard'
'P.T.A. (Parent Teacher Association)'
'Razzmatazz'
'Seductive Barry'
'Sheffield: Sex City'
'Something Changed'

'Sorted for E's & Wizz'
'Space'
'Stacks'
'Street Lites'
'The Babysitter'
'The Fear'
'The Last Day of the Miners' Strike'
'The Professional'
'The Quiet Revolution'
'The Trees'
'This Is Hardcore'
'TV Movie'
'Weeds II (The Origin of the Species)'
'Wickerman'
Reproduced by kind permission Universal/Island Music Ltd

'B-Real'
'Mary'
'Set the Controls for the Heart of the Pelvis'
Reproduced by kind permission Universal/Island Music Ltd
and Mute Song

'Cocaine Socialism'
'Glory Days'
'Sliding Through Life on Charm'
Reproduced by kind permission of Universal/Island Music
Ltd and EMI Music Publishing

'First Man in Space'
'Stars on Sunday'
Reproduced by kind permission of Universal/Island Music
Ltd and Chrysalis Music Ltd

'Big Julie'
'Cunts Are Still Running the World'